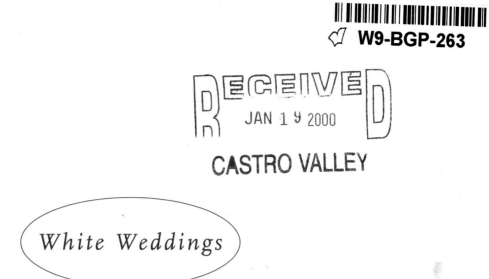

White Weddings

White Weddings

Romancing Heterosexuality in Popular Culture

Chrys Ingraham

Routledge
New York & London

Published in 1999 by
Routledge
29 West 35th Street
New York, NY 10001

Published in Great Britain by
Routledge
11 New Fetter Lane
London EC4P 4EE

Copyright © 1999 by Routledge

Printed in the United States of America on acid-free paper.

Library of Congress Cataloging-in-Publication Data
Ingraham, Chrys, 1947–
White weddings : romancing heterosexuality in
popular culture / by Chrys Ingraham.
p. cm.
Includes bibliographical references.
ISBN 0-415-91839-1 (hc.).—ISBN 0-415-91840-5 (pbk.)
1. Marriage—United States. 2. Weddings—United States.
3. Weddings in popular culture—United States.
4. Heterosexuality—United States. I. Title.
HQ536.I545 1999
392.5'0973—dc21   98-54134
CIP

To my parents

for providing many
of life's lessons

And to all those
children and adults
whose labor
and imaginations
are too great a price
for our comfort.

Wedding photo, 1946

Contents

Acknowledgments

This book is the product of the biggest "unwedding" ever assembled! The unwedding reception was enormous and the costs were mostly intellectual, emotional, and spiritual, but the gifts offered by so many were beyond compare. Etched into the pages of this manuscript are the fingerprints, coffee stains, ink, dog hairs, and love of many who helped to bring this to reality. To all who helped put on this critical spectacle, I owe an enormous amount of gratitude.

This book came to fruition in large part because of the enormously caring and collaborative contributions of friends, coworkers, family, and students who have touched, coaxed, coached, and inspired it into existence. My gratitude to all exceeds my ability to find the right words.

First and foremost, I'd like to thank *all* of my students, both past and present. Their energy, idealism, and intellectual curiosity have motivated me to keep questioning. In particular, I'd like to acknowledge the efforts of Russell Sage College students Ayisha Amjad, Annuola Austin, Rachele Bauer, Carrie Cokely, Jennifer Madison, Erin Maher, Likkia Moody, Michelle Schultz, and Janelle Yielding. I'd also like to recognize the significant contributions made by Ithaca College students who rose to the challenge and brought these ideas to life in a course called Marriage and Family: Critical Perspectives.

Special thanks to Pat Behan for lightening my load and for managing some of the most tiresome tasks with the greatest care and efficiency. I don't know what I would have done without you.

To my friend and "coach," Linnea Jatulis, who said, "Every week we're going to devote time to a progress report on your book! This has to get written!" Thanks to her confidence, insight, friendship, phone calls, and critical readings, that's exactly what happened. I'm honored to call this woman my friend and I'm delighted that her fingerprints cover this text.

And to another generous friend, Joni Dacher, who offered endless support, phone messages of encouragement, and who served as insightful reader and muse during some low points, I am enormously grateful.

Tonia Blackwell, the "best ally" a woman can have, spent countless hours "theorizin" and commiserating with me about the trials and tribulations of life, politics, romance, and social change. Our laughter, tears, and hard work together inform much of this work.

So many others commiserated, cajoled, comforted, influenced, and loved me through this project. My deepest gratitude to: Lisa Callahan, Lisa Carr, Paige Carr-Tutt, Mildred Dandridge, Marj DeVault, Jayne Fargnoli, Marilyn Gewacke, David Goldenberg, Kay Gormley, Leslie Grout, Mindy Jatulis, Carla Jones, Judy Long, Julia Loughlin, Libby Mahoney, Julie McIntyre, Maureen McLeod, David Milford, Teresa Pistolessi, Sharon Robinson, Bronna Romanoff, Andor Skotnes, Mike Sposili, Maren Stein, Leyla Vural, Peggy Walsh, and Mary Ellen Wogan. And to the Dominoes Group, who reminded us all what it means to work and play well together.

I owe a debt of gratitude to Steven Seidman, friend, colleague, and mentor, who gave my article on this topic its first airing in *Sociological Theory* and again in his collection of essays *Queer Theory/Sociology*.

The resources and assistance of many staff people and administrators at Russell Sage College have been very helpful. In particular, I'd like to thank the workers in Interlibrary Loan for their outstanding contribution, and the "guys"—Mike, Scott, and Mark—at the Service Center. The Eastern Sociological Society and the American Sociological Association also contributed to this outcome by providing a productive environment for the presentation of many of the ideas presented here.

My family has been the single greatest source of life's lessons. To all of them I am deeply grateful for the opportunities and love they have provided: June Ingraham, Laurie James, Mark Ingraham, Loren James, Jason and Jill Kantak, Chris Kantak, Molly and Kate Hennessy-Fiske, Mary Beth Ingraham, Matthew James, and Adam James.

My engagement with this project began many years ago in a community of activists in

Syracuse, N.Y., where I learned to appreciate the labor of love required for turning rage into action. For teaching so many how to reach out beyond the illusion of romance to create a more humane and loving world I want to acknowledge Jane Hugo, Donna Inglima, Mary Ellen Kavanaugh, Karen Mihalyi, Diane Ogno, Lesley Pease, Deborah Pellow, Toni Taverone, Hope Wallis, and Syracuse Cultural Workers.

When we imagine a world where celebrations of love go beyond the type discussed in this study, Maureen Casey and Brian O'Shaughnessy are two people whose work for peace and justice should be among the first we honor. For the beautiful space you shared, the solace and strength you provided, I am deeply grateful. And to Jim and Ellen O'Shaughnessy whose generosity provided the solitude and comfort that made this task less arduous.

To my heart sisters and shooting stars, Sue Hillery and Layne Hamilton, thank you for traveling with me through all that life brings and for encouraging and sustaining me through this project. Where would I be today without you? I can't imagine.

This book would have taken a lot longer had it not been for the love and friendship of Lisa Koogle. Her steadfast and generous heart, caring words, undying confidence, loving support, occasional kick in the ass, high tolerance for whining, and great sense of humor have carried me through some of the best and hardest moments. I am deeply thankful for your many gifts.

Where would this book be today without my new Jewish mother, editor, and muse, Ilene Kalish? Thank you for being the joyful, encouraging, and brilliant voice on the other end of the phone and for believing in this project. I never cease to be impressed by your talents—and I don't know what I would have done without that laugh and those "cheap" Italian dinners!

And to Rosemary Hennessy for working with me to expand the boundaries of acceptability, understanding, and change. You've pushed me to stretch in ways I could never have imagined on my own—intellectually, politically, and emotionally. Your insights and wisdom are woven into the very fabric of these pages. For all you've given, thank you.

I'd like to think that this project honors the memory of some of the greatest guides I've known: Lulu Gamblin, Bea Spaulding, Toni Taverone, Earl Watchorn, Chris Youngberg, and my Dad for correcting my grammar and spelling and for lighting the way.

Chapter One

Lifting the Veil

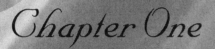

Driving from Ithaca to Albany one spring night in 1992 I heard a report on National Public Radio's *All Things Considered* about the fact that thirteen TV shows were ending their season with weddings. Ever the alert sociologist, I exclaimed out loud to the radio, "Wow! What's that all about?" Since I frequently teach courses on social inequality, marriage and family, and women's studies, I was more than idly curious. In the weeks that followed I watched some of these shows and became conscious of the degree to which weddings—especially *white* weddings—permeate popular culture. White weddings were not only main fare on situation comedies but were also used to sell everything from antacids to soap. Even when they weren't the central theme they were inserted into the background. Television, however, was not the only medium in which this trend was visible. The movie industry appeared to be capitalizing on the same theme, particularly after the 1991 success of *Father of the Bride*, a remake of the classic 1950s version, using weddings as the main theme or as a plot device somewhere in the film.

When I turned to research journals for help in understanding what was going on, I was surprised again. While sociologists have produced a significant body of research on marriage, no U.S. sociologist has ever published a study on weddings. In fact, with the exception of a Canadian sociologist who also wonders why weddings haven't been studied (Currie 1993), they are rarely examined in any academic discipline. This glaring omission seemed particularly stunning in relation to the pervasiveness of both the practice and its presence in popular culture. I was left with several questions: Why are weddings receiving all this attention from the media? How can they be so present in popular culture yet so absent from scrutiny? Do we take them for granted to such an extent that we don't notice that they merit study? Or do we understand them to be of so little importance that we assume there is nothing to be learned from studying them? And why *white* weddings? What is the significance of the white wedding?

This book will show that there is *much* we can learn from a close examination of weddings. *White Weddings: Romancing Heterosexuality in Popular Culture* is one of the first studies of weddings in American culture. White weddings, as the dominant wedding form, permeate both the culture and the industry. Specifically, the stereotypical white wedding is a spectacle featuring a bride in a formal white wedding gown, combined with some combination of attendants and witnesses, religious ceremony, wedding reception, and honeymoon.

This study provides some insights into the ways weddings are used to define the operation of heterosexuality in U.S. media and popular culture. Given that weddings have served as a symbolic rite of passage for heterosexual men and women entering marriage, one of the most important outcomes of this study is what it reveals about how heterosexuality is *institutionalized*.

Typically studied as a form of sexuality, heterosexuality is, in reality, a highly regulated, ritualized, and organized practice. Sociologically, then, heterosexuality as an "established order made up of rule-bound and standardized behavior patterns" (Jary and Jary 1991, 239) qualifies as an institution. Moreover, heterosexuality as an "arrangement involving large numbers of people whose behavior is guided by norms and rules" (Jary and Jary 1991, 239) is also a *social* institution. In other words, heterosexuality is much more than a biological given or the fact that someone is or is not attracted to someone of the other sex. "Naturally" occurring or

"It's the only formal party some people are ever invited to. It's the only couture dress many women will ever own. It's the only catered event many people ever attend. There's no mystery to why people love weddings and are thrilled to sit through them again and again. And in today's popular culture, geared to pander and give the people what they want and only what they want, audiences are getting plenty of opportunity to sit through weddings. Again and again."

—Amy M. Spindler, "The Wedding Dress That Ate Hollywood," the *New York Times*, Sunday Styles, August 30, 1998: 9.1

3

not, heterosexuality is highly organized by society and by culture. While you may argue that "heterosexuality is natural" or that you were " just born this way," women didn't enter this world knowing they wanted to wear a prom dress, practice something called "dating," buy a white wedding gown, or play with a "My Size Bride Barbie." Likewise, men did not exit the womb knowing they would one day have to buy a date a corsage or spend two months' income to buy an engagement ring. Rules on everything from who pays for the date or the rehearsal dinner to who leads while dancing, drives the car, cooks dinner, or initiates sex all serve to regulate heterosexual practice. What circulates as a given in American society is, in fact, a highly structured arrangement. As is the case with most institutions, people who participate in these practices must be *socialized* to do so. *Weddings are one of the major events that signal readiness and prepare heterosexuals for membership in marriage as an organizing practice for the institution of heterosexuality.* Evidence for this can be seen in the magnitude of the wedding industry.

The Wedding Industry

Weddings are big money, and everyone wants to get in on the act. Bridal gown stores are mainstays in most cities and towns regardless of size; giant bridal shows are held several times a year in major cities; wedding consultants abound; popular magazines feature special wedding issues; paparazzi risk life and limb to get photos of celebrity weddings; television commercials and popular films incorporate them; soap operas and romance novels depend upon them; home video and bloopers shows feature wedding gaffs; thrift stores showcase bridal gowns; discount stores offer bride and groom cake tops; and toy stores sell everything from bridal dolls to wedding toys. Just look around and you'll see how pervasively weddings appear in American culture.

The wedding industry, where the average American couple spends $19,104 per wedding (*Bride's* 1997), thrives in large part because it serves approximately 2.45 million couples per year (U.S. Bureau of the Census 1996).[1] While the bridal gown industry is experiencing a mild recession, largely due to changes in marketing and dress manufacturing, its customers still spend an average of $823 on a wedding

Woman with
wedding cake hat

gown and an additional $166 on headpiece and veil ($989 total) (*Bride's* 1997).
When you consider these trends in relation to income levels across various groups,
it becomes evident that the wedding market is not addressed to or available to
everyone.

Weddings are no longer confined to the so-called "Bride" pages of local and
national newspapers; they have become a mainstay of American popular culture.
While the 1992 television season ended with weddings, the 1997–98 season
opened, in *Dharma & Greg*, and closed with them, in *Friends, The Nanny, Jag, Spin
City, Baywatch, Suddenly Susan, Dr. Quinn, Everybody Loves Raymond, NYPD Blue,*

Dennis Rodman in
bridal gown

and *For Your Love*. And, in case you thought that would be enough, *TV Guide's Fall Preview '98* issue announced "*Friends* Wedding Scandal Revealed!" as *Friends* opens with the conclusion of the wedding that ended the previous season. Sitcoms *To Have & To Hold* and *Will & Grace* begin in 1998–99 with weddings; the made-for-television movies *Forever Love, The Marriage Fool, A Marriage of Convenience,* and *I Married a Monster* all feature a wedding. Weddings are regularly featured on "bloopers" shows and frequently appear in television commercials for everything from Aleve to Metropolitan Life Insurance to ads for chain saws, real estate, long-distance service, and cars. As for soap operas, long a source of romance drama,

Museum of the City of New York

invites you to attend

a special exhibition

New York Gets Married

Dressing for a Special Day, 1765-1997

May 21, 1997 through September 21, 1997

Museum of the City of New York

1220 Fifth Avenue at 103rd Street

(212) 534-1672

Sponsored by Tiffany & Co.

Reprint of New York
Museum invitation

General Hospital claims the most viewership of daytime television for the wedding episode of Luke and Laura. Daytime talk shows from *Live! With Regis and Kathie Lee* to *Oprah* to *Montel Williams* regularly dedicate shows or even entire weeks of shows to wedding products or to the presentation of actual weddings. Toy manufacturers have also seized on the current wedding market and the opportunity to develop future consumers by producing a whole new variety of wedding toys which feature prominently in Saturday-morning children's television shows and advertising. The Lifetime Channel regularly features "Celebrity Weddings," and The Learning Channel sponsors an hour-long show on real weddings every weekday afternoon opposite soap operas on other channels.

Today, it's practically impossible to walk through any grocery store or by any checkout counter without being inundated with romance novels, magazines and tabloids on various celebrity or soap opera weddings, or wedding how-to and fashion magazines. In July 1993, *People* magazine, considered by many to be one of the most successful magazines of our time, added a yearly celebrity-wedding special issue to its lineup. It has become "the magazine's best-selling special issue with over four million copies sold" (Zuber 1994, p. 70). Martha Stewart has recently entered the wedding magazine and retail market with special wedding issues of *Living*. Mail-order catalogs regularly devote pages to wedding products, and bookstores offer numerous volumes for planning the "perfect" wedding. Even computer shareware and software programs feature wedding planners for the bride- and groom-to-be.

In the past few years we have witnessed the enormous success of wedding films such as *The Birdcage, The Wedding Banquet, Father of the Bride, Four Weddings and a Funeral* (nominated for an Oscar for best picture), *Muriel's Wedding, My Best Friend's Wedding, In & Out, Polish Wedding,* and *The Wedding Singer.* Forthcoming from the director of *Pretty Woman,* Garry Marshall, are two films, one that reunites Richard Gere and Julia Roberts entitled *Runaway Bride* and another, *The Other Sister,* with Diane Keaton and Juliette Lewis, which has two weddings in it. While these productions have been on the rise, the movie industry has also managed to include a wedding in most films even when the story line seems unrelated, e.g., *Armaggedon* saves the world for two white weddings. Clearly, weddings have become the most watched yet "unnoticed" phenomenon in popular culture.

That there has been little or no serious study of weddings given the findings of this study is not surprising. The social, political, and economic investment in heterosexuality as it is currently organized holds great consequence for much of what we've come to hold sacred and personal. How we've come to understand these things is the subject of this book.

Setting the Context

Given the size and significance of the practice, why have researchers overlooked weddings and the study of heterosexuality *as an institution*? One possible explanation may be the risk involved in pursuing such an examination. Efforts to critically examine many sacred or valued practices and institutions are frequently resisted and suppressed. Readers may employ typical suppressionary strategies by reacting to such discussions as personal attacks on themselves or on heterosexuals as a group rather than as institutional analyses or inventories. Such practices are commonplace in analytical discussions of such issues as racism or classism.

As activists in the nineteenth century discovered, to critically examine heterosexuality's rules and norms was to encounter either legal or social sanction. For example, marriage reform activists were often censored and jailed under the Comstock Act of 1872. As part of the free thinker movement, activists dedicated themselves to the elimination of church and state control over marriage, arguing that under these rules marriage was a form of "sexual slavery" (Harman 1883). When these marriage reformers attempted to distribute their ideas, they were frequently arrested, indicted, and convicted for mailing "obscene" materials through the U.S. Postal Service. To mail writings on "sex education, birth control, or abortion" was deemed by U.S. Postal Code 1461—the Comstock Act—as the dissemination of obscenity and a federal offense. The following three cases (out of nearly thirty-seven hundred) are some of the most prominent examples of the censorship of marriage critique and reform.

First and most famous was the censorship of Ezra Heywood's published treatise, *Cupid's Yokes* (1876).[2] In it Heywood critiqued marriage as a form of legalized prostitution, arguing that women, as the property of men, were forced to provide sexual and reproductive services in exchange for economic support and security. This powerful tract was widely distributed and censored twice. Nevertheless, Heywood persisted in trying to pressure the inequities of marriage.

In another notable instance, Moses Harman, publisher of a free thinker newspaper, printed a letter from a reader documenting the death of a woman who had been raped by her husband immediately following childbirth.[3] Because she was the man's wife, no legal action was taken against him. The husband escaped punishment, but Harman's newspaper was impounded and he was sentenced to prison for publishing the letter.

Marital rape was a problem being addressed by several individuals during this period. One of the best-kept secrets among white, middle-class families was the shock experienced by women on their wedding night. Uneducated about sexual intercourse, many young brides were traumatized by the experience. With the rise of the medical profession, social reformers sought to remedy this situation by publishing books and articles addressed to young women, educating them about sex. One such person was Ida Craddock, who published and distributed through the mail a small book called *The Wedding Night*. Craddock's case was particularly tragic. Having already served one sentence under horrendous prison conditions, Craddock chose death as less traumatic than prison when she was prosecuted the second time. Her last effort at public protest was the publication of her suicide letter in a local newspaper, in which she claimed the last word in her fight against Anthony Comstock and the injustice of the law he zealously enforced. The chilling effect these acts of censorship had on the marriage reform movement were significant enough to silence these debates for decades. Even today, few people are aware of either this social movement or of its martyrs. Not until the 1960s did similar discussions reemerge.

Late-twentieth-century feminists such as the Furies Collective, Purple September Staff, Redstockings (1975), Rita Mae Brown (1976), and Charlotte Bunch (1975) challenged dominant notions of heterosexuality as naturally occurring and argued that it is instead a highly organized social institution rife with multiple forms of domination and ideological control. In this excerpt from Charlotte Bunch, the link between heterosexuality and systems of oppression is elaborated:

> Heterosexuality—as an ideology and as an institution—upholds all those
> aspects of female oppression. . . . For example, heterosexuality is basic
> to our oppression in the workplace. When we look at how women are
> defined and exploited as secondary, marginal workers, we recognize
> that this definition assumes that all women are tied to men. . . . It is

> obvious that heterosexuality upholds the home, housework, the family
> as both a personal and economic unit. (Bunch 1975, 34)

While many of these arguments were made by heterosexually identified feminists, some of the more famous works were produced by lesbian feminists, making a link to the interests of both feminism and lesbian and gay rights. Adrienne Rich's frequently reprinted essay "Compulsory Heterosexuality and Lesbian Existence" (1980) confronts the institution of heterosexuality head on, asserting that heterosexuality is neither natural nor inevitable but is instead a "compulsory," contrived, constructed, and taken-for-granted institution that serves the interests of male dominance.

> Historians need to ask at every point how heterosexuality as an
> institution has been organized and maintained through the female wage
> scale, the enforcement of middle-class women's "leisure," the
> glamorization of so-called sexual liberation, the withholding of
> education from women, the imagery of "high art" and popular culture,
> the mystification of the "personal" sphere, and much else. We need an
> economics which comprehends the institution of heterosexuality, with
> its doubled workload for women and its sexual divisions of labor, as the
> most idealized of economic relations. (27)

Understanding heterosexuality as an institution with processes and effects is one of Rich's greatest contributions.

Monique Wittig's "The Category of Sex" (1992) takes the argument to a different level, declaring heterosexuality a political regime.

> The category of sex is the political category that founds society as
> heterosexual. As such it does not concern being but relationships. . . .
> The category of sex is the one that rules as "natural" the relation that is
> at the base of (heterosexual) society and through which half of the
> population, women, are "heterosexualized" . . . and submitted to a

> heterosexual economy. . . . The category of sex is the product of a
> heterosexual society in which men appropriate for themselves the
> reproduction and production of women and also their physical persons
> by means of a contract called the marriage contract. (1992, p 7)

And this regime depends upon the belief that women are "sexual beings," unable to escape or live outside of male rule.

All of these essays provide the foundation for a sustained and critical evaluation of institutionalized heterosexuality, one that allows for a level of awareness that is both liberating and transformative.

Twenty-five years later, these works have, for the most part disappeared (out of sight, out of mind), as the backlash against such challenges has intensified. References to "femi-nazis" and political correctness and gay-baiting tactics have been used as powerful suppression strategies to once again create a climate hostile to most attempts to constructively critique the ways gender and institutionalized heterosexuality operate and oppress. In fact, it has become so extreme that efforts to assign several seemingly benign biographies of women as texts for first-year college students have been met with the same backlash rhetoric.[4] Similiar to the red-baiting strategies of the Cold War period, where any attempt to inquire into the operation of capitalism was met with anticommunist backlash, various suppressionary tactics are being used to thwart and discredit any critical discussion of heterosexuality. Instead, flimsy research on the biological basis of sexuality appears as an unquestioned scientific milestone in the mainstream media, leaving the impression that difference in sexual orientation can finally be explained by biology. *One effect of these social forces is that institutionalized heterosexuality remains unexamined and invisible.*

Because of its central role in society, heterosexuality is in a continual state of crisis and contradiction as pressures from a range of historical and material conditions shift and change. For example, pressures from feminism, from the lesbian/gay/bisexual/transgendered rights movement, the sexual revolution of the

1960s and 1970s, and the prevalence of AIDS as a life-threatening sexually transmitted disease have altered the taken-for-granted beliefs/ideologies about sexuality, gender, and marriage. A rising divorce rate (4.6 out of 10 marriages end in divorce; in the case of African Americans the number is 6 out of 10), increases in domestic and sexual violence (1 out of 6 women is a victim of domestic violence; 44 percent of women murdered in the United States are killed by their male partner or ex-partner (U.S. Census Bureau 1996; Federal Domestic Violence Statistics 1998), the proliferation of single parenthood, and the absence of jobs, women's employment, day care, and job training all have worked to destabilize institutionalized heterosexuality. Of all these, women's increasing economic independence may be the single most important reason for marriage's increasing irrelevance. Income distribution for both men and women has changed enough in recent decades to necessitate that both partners work outside the home. Marriage—formerly thought of as a structure that guarantees a male breadwinner whose primary role is to support a wife and children—no longer holds the same historical necessity. Now, both incomes support the household.

Definitions of heterosexuality have been shifting significantly in areas targeted specifically to teenagers and young adults. MTV has had enormous impact in this area, since it frequently presents shows, videos, and ads providing alternative views of heterosexuality as well as proactive views of gays and lesbians, such as rock icons Melissa Etheridge and Elton John. The 1997–98 television season offered the first openly gay sitcom star and character in *Ellen*, portrayed by Ellen DeGeneres. The show was later canceled in part due to controversy over (frequently political) gay content. The Emmy award-winning series *Mad About You* closed out its 1997–98 season with an episode in which Paul's sister and her lesbian partner professed their love and commitment to each other and decided to wed. They sealed this "engagement" with a kiss on prime-time television. Critically acclaimed box office hits—movies such as *Four Weddings and a Funeral*, *The Crying Game*, *In & Out*, *The Birdcage*, and *The Wedding Banquet*—have all pressured dominant notions of heterosexuality through the insertion of either transgendered or lesbian/gay normalizing themes.

In opposition to these growing trends, several powerful groups—the New Right,

In a recent article in the New York Times *(3/23/98), it was reported that Christian conservatives will pressure the Republican Party to "put issues like abortion, sexual morality and family values in the forefront of every campaign. . . ." In reference to this new push, one conservative leader commented, "No more engagement. We want a wedding ring, we want a ceremony, we want a consummation of the marriage."*

the Christian Coalition, right-to-lifers, conservative Republicans, Dittoheads (Rush Limbaugh followers), Southern Baptists, and Promise Keepers—have actively campaigned to secure patriarchal heterosexuality (male-dominated as opposed to egalitarian) as dominant. Through moves designed to discredit any practices that do not privilege this arrangement while reclaiming and rewarding those that honor it, these interests have launched a full-scale national attack on any group—whether it be lesbians, gays, single mothers, domestic partners, or transgendered people—which does not subscribe to the dominant heterosexual arrangement. Their strategy focuses on two fronts: the legal (as evidenced by pervasive national attacks on gay rights and gay marriage legislation) and the ideological (propaganda campaigns against gays and lesbians). The most recent of these is the current "homosexual conversion" ad campaign, funded by religious and political conservatives, which purports to "change" homosexuals to heterosexuals through devotion to Jesus.

In various sites within popular culture, the reassertion of dominance is most evident in the proliferation of one of heterosexuality's key organizing rituals, the wedding. This romance with wedding culture works ideologically to naturalize the regulation of sexuality through the institution of marriage, providing images or representations of reality that mask the historical and material conditions of life. Consider, for example, how weddings in popular culture are being used to manage the current crisis in capitalism and patriarchy.

In 1997, as the U.S. Congress grappled with the now infamous Republican Contract with America, arguments over welfare reform escalated. Politicians and conservative interest groups launched a full-scale campaign against the "unmarried welfare mother." The "welfare queen," a stereotype made famous by Ronald Reagan, has been newly revived in a variety of images throughout popular culture. It is the image of the welfare mother as African-American, unmarried, urban, probably under eighteen, caught in a life-long cycle of poverty, and single parent to many small children born "out of *wed*lock." This stereotype prevails despite the fact that the average welfare recipient is white, has been on welfare for less than two years, and has fewer than two children and collects benefits for less than two years. Incorporated within this stereotype is the view that these are women and children who have become dependent upon welfare and have never done the responsible thing—get married. To correct what has been identified as a drain on federal and state budgets and the future health of the American economy, federal and state politicians have advanced policy proposals recommending *marriage* as the primary vehicle for both recovery from welfare dependency and from a federal deficit. When welfare spending amounted to only 1.2 percent of the gross domestic product in 1992 and federal welfare spending amounted to about 5 percent of the federal budget, one wonders how this focus on the marital responsibility of the poor will correct the trillion-dollar national debt (President's Council 1992, 1994). In this same historical moment, the wedding-industrial complex, made up of hundreds of companies directly and indirectly engaged in the wedding industry, is thriving, to the tune of $32 billion per year.

As debates over budgets and deficits continue, downsizing has become a dominant corporate strategy affecting millions of workers throughout the U.S., the class divide between the rich and the poor is the widest in decades, welfare reform and workfare have become law, CEOs are earning record levels of income and wealth, labor is being compromised in a range of sites, and transnational corporations and sweatshops (inside and outside the U.S.) are proliferating. At the same time, the wedding industry is thriving, and weddings in popular culture are presenting the promise of accumulation and wealth. The following section explains the theory and mode of inquiry used to examine institutionalized heterosexuality through the study of weddings in popular culture.

The Heterosexual Imaginary: What Are the Conditions That Allow Us to Imagine Possibilities?

To pursue a study of weddings requires a theory and a methodology capable of confronting the invisibility of the institution of heterosexuality while opening up an awareness and understanding of its operation, particularly in such practices as the white wedding. French psychoanalyst Jacques Lacan's concept of the "imaginary" is useful for this purpose. He described the imaginary as the unmediated contact an infant has to its own image and its connection with its mother. Instead of facing a complicated, conflictual, and contradictory world, the infant experiences the illusion of tranquility, plenitude, and fullness. Louis Althusser, the French philosopher, borrowed Lacan's notion of the imaginary for his theory of ideology, defining ideology as "the imaginary relationship of individuals to their real conditions of existence" (1971, 52). The "imaginary" here does not mean "false" or "pretend" but, rather, an imagined relationship between the individual and the world. The *heterosexual* imaginary[5] is that way of thinking that conceals the operation of heterosexuality in structuring gender (across race, class, and sexuality) and closes off any critical analysis of heterosexuality as an organizing institution (Ingraham 1994). It is a belief system that relies on romantic and sacred notions of heterosexuality in order to create and maintain the illusion of well-being. At the same time this romantic view prevents us from seeing how institutionalized heterosexuality actually works to organize gender while preserving racial, class, and sexual hierarchies as well. The effect of this illusory depiction of reality is that heterosexuality is taken for granted and unquestioned while gender is understood as something people are socialized into or learn. By leaving heterosexuality unexamined as an institution we don't explore how it is learned, what it keeps in place, and the interests it serves in the way it's currently practiced. Through the use of the heterosexual imaginary, we hold up the institution of heterosexuality as timeless, devoid of historical variation, and as "just the way it is" while creating social practices that reinforce the illusion that as long as this is "the way it is" all will be right in the world. Romancing—creating an illusory—heterosexuality is central to the heterosexual imaginary.

Meanwhile, some of the consequences the heterosexual imaginary produces are anything but tranquil or safe, for example, marital rape, domestic violence, pay inequities, racism, gay bashing, and sexual harassment. Instead, institutionalized heterosexuality organizes those behaviors we ascribe to men and women—gender—while keeping in place or producing a history of contradictory and unequal social relations. The production of a division of labor that results in unpaid domestic work, inequalities of pay and opportunity, or the privileging of married couples in the dissemination of insurance benefits are examples of this. Above all, the heterosexual imaginary naturalizes the regulation of sexuality through the institution of marriage and state domestic relations laws. These laws, among others, set the terms for taxation, health care, and housing benefits on the basis of marital status. Rarely challenged—except by nineteenth-century marriage reformers and early second-wave feminists[6]—laws and public- and private-sector policies use marriage as the primary requirement for social and economic benefits and access rather than distributing resources on some other basis such as citizenship or ability to breathe, for example. With so much at stake, it's easy to see why weddings as the symbolic entrance into marriage take on such importance.

Another useful concept for a study of weddings is heteronormativity. This is the view that institutionalized heterosexuality constitutes the standard for legitimate and expected social and sexual relations. Heteronormativity represents one of the main premises underlying the heterosexual imaginary, again ensuring that the organization of heterosexuality in everything from gender to weddings to marital status is held up as both a model and as "normal." Consider, for instance, the ways many surveys or intake questionnaires ask respondents to check off their marital status as either married, divorced, separated, widowed, single, or, in some cases, never married. Not only are these categories presented as significant indices of social identity, they are offered as the only options, implying that the organization of identity in relation to marriage is universal and not in need of explanation. Questions concerning marital status appear on most surveys regardless of relevance. The heteronormative assumption of this practice is rarely, if ever, called into question, and when it is, the response is generally dismissive. (Try putting down "not applicable" the next time you fill out one of these forms in a doctor's office!) Heteronormativity works in this instance to naturalize the institution of heterosexuality.

For those who view questions concerning marital status as benign, one need only consider the social and economic consequences for those respondents who do not participate in these arrangements or the cross-cultural variations that are at odds with some of the Anglocentric or Eurocentric assumptions regarding marriage. All respondents are invited to situate themselves in relation to marriage or heterosexuality, including those who *regardless of sexual (or asexual) affiliation* do not consider themselves "single" or heterosexual, or who think of themselves as the unimaginable: not participating in these arrangements.

To study weddings using this theory of heterosexuality is to investigate the ways various practices, arrangements, relations, and rituals work to conceal the operation of this institution. It means to ask how practices such as weddings prevent us from seeing what is at stake, what is kept in place, and what consequences are produced. To employ this approach is to seek out those instances when the illusion of tranquility is created and at what cost. Weddings, like many other rituals of heterosexual celebration such as anniversaries, showers, and Valentine's Day, provide images of reality that conceal the operation of heterosexuality both historically and materially. When used in professional settings, for example, weddings work as a form of ideological control to signal membership in relations of ruling[7] as well as to signify that the couple is normal, moral, productive, family-centered, upstanding, and, most importantly, appropriately gendered. Consider the ways weddings are used by coworkers in line for promotions or to marginalize and exceptionalize single or nonmarried employees. For example, two employees are competing for a promotion. One is single, the other engaged to marry. The engaged worker invites all members of the office, including the hiring committee, to the wedding. Because of the heterosexual imaginary, weddings are viewed as innocuous, fun-loving, and as signaling membership in dominant culture. As such, they give people significant advantage in the workplace and are anything but benign.

To undertake a study of marriage is to interrupt the ways the heterosexual imaginary naturalizes heterosexuality and prevents us from seeing how its organization depends on the production of the belief or ideology that heterosexuality is the same for everyone—that the fairy-tale romance is universal. This type of study requires a form of systemic analysis of the ways both the institution of heterosexuality and the heterosexual imaginary, particularly in relation to weddings, are historically bound up in the distribution of economic resources, cultural power, and social control. To this end I will make use of a materialist feminist mode of inquiry.

Materialist Feminism

Materialist feminism as a mode of inquiry begins with an analytic capable of revealing taken-for-granted social arrangements, e.g., weddings, and exposing the economic, political, and ideological conditions upon which they depend. By *materialism* I am referring here to the division of labor and the distribution of wealth (private property) in the context of historically prevailing national and state interests and ideological struggles over meaning and value.

Materialist feminism argues that the nexus of social arrangements and institutions that form the social totalities of patriarchy and capitalism regulate our everyday lives by distributing cultural power and economic resources unevenly according to gender, race, class, and sexuality. Within this framework, rape and domestic violence, for example, can be seen as the effect of social structures and processes that situate men hierarchically in relation to women and to each other. Historically, this has been accomplished using forms of social differentiation such as heterosexuality, with its historically specific heterogendered—that is, the asymmetrical stratification of the sexes in relation to the historically varying institutions of patriarchal heterosexuality—and racial components.

Applying a materialist feminist analytic to capitalism means examining it as a regime for 1) the production of surplus value (profit); 2) the securing of private property (accumulation); 3) the exploitation and alienation of life and labor; 4) the division and distribution of labor and wealth; 5) global and state interests; and 6) those meaning-making systems that reproduce capitalism and patriarchy. A materialist feminist approach also understands that capitalism operates under varying historical, regional, and global conditions of existence. For instance, capitalism in Japan is not the same as capitalism in the United States, even though the systems are interrelated and reciprocal and produce similar effects. They emerge from different historical and material relations of production and therefore defy reductive generalization. To study white weddings in the U.S. using a materialist feminist analytic, then, would not necessarily be generalizable to other cultures.

Patriarchy is also historically variable, producing a hierarchy of heterogender[8] divisions that privilege men as a group and exploit women as a group. Patriarchy structures social practices that it represents as natural and universal and that are reinforced by its organizing institutions and rituals (e.g., marriage and weddings). As a totality, patriarchy organizes difference by positioning men in hierarchical opposition to women and differentially in relation to other structures, such as race

19

Scriptural reading from a wedding ceremony held June 20, 1998:

Wives, submit yourselves unto your husbands, as unto the Lord.

For the husband is head of the wife, even as Christ is the head of the church: and he is the savior of the body.

Therefore as the church is subject unto Christ, so let the wives be to their own husbands in every thing.

Husbands, love your wives, even as Christ also love the church, and gave himself for it;

That he might present it to himself a glorious church, not having spot, or wrinkle, or any such thing; but that it should be holy and without blemish.

So ought men to love their wives as their own bodies. He that loveth his wife loveth himself.

For no man ever yet hated his own flesh; but nourisheth and cherisheth it, even as the Lord the church:

For we are members of his body, of his flesh, and of his bones.

For this cause shall a man leave his father and mother, and shall be joined unto his wife, and they two shall be one flesh.

This is the great mystery: but I speak concerning Christ and the church.

Nevertheless let every one of you in particular so love his wife even as himself; and the wife see that she reverence her husband.

Ephesians 5:22–33

or class. Its continued success depends on the maintenance of regimes of difference as well as on a range of material forces. It is a totality that not only varies cross-nationally, but also manifests differently across ethnic, racial, and class boundaries within nations. For instance, patriarchy in African-American culture differs significantly from patriarchy in other groups in U.S. society. Even though each group shares certain understandings of hierarchical relations between men and women, the historical relation of African-American men to African-American women is dramatically different from that among Anglo-European Americans. Among African Americans, a group that has suffered extensively from white supremacist policies and practices, solidarity as a "racial" group has frequently superseded asymmetrical divisions based on heterogender. This is not to say that patriarchal relations do not exist among African Americans, but that they have manifested differently among racial-ethnic groups as a result of historical necessity. Interestingly, racism has sometimes emerged in relation to criticisms of African-American men for not being patriarchal enough by Euro-American standards. As a totality, patriarchy produces structural effects that situate men differently in relation to women and to each other according to history.

Applying a materialist feminist mode of inquiry to the study of white weddings in popular culture means examining various texts such as the *New York Times* wedding pages, bridal magazines, television sitcoms, films, and children's toys for their foundational assumptions. It means determining what is concealed or excluded in relation to what is presumed or presented. This mode of inquiry, then, makes visible the "permitted" meanings—what the culture allows us to say—in constructions of weddings, marriage, and ultimately, heterosexuality. What is required, then, is a process of analysis capable of inquiring into the power relations organizing the allowed as well as the disallowed meanings in an effort to expose the use of particular concepts.

Materialist feminist ideology critique seeks to demystify the ways in which dominant or ruling-class beliefs are authorized and inscribed in subjectivities (what it means to be a woman, a wife, a bride, or a mother), institutional arrangements (marriage), and various cultural narratives (films, magazines, television, and ads). Like those taken-for-granted beliefs, values, and assumptions encoded as power relations within social texts and practices, ideology is central to the reproduction of a social order. Because it produces what is allowed to count as reality, ideology constitutes a material force and at the same time is shaped by other economic and political forces. This theory of ideology addresses the meaning-making processes embedded within any social practice, including the production of wedding and marriage culture.

Inherently contradictory, capitalist and patriarchal social arrangements are in a continual state of crisis management. The work of dominant ideologies, such as romantic love, is to conceal these contradictions in order to maintain the social order. At the same time, however, these breaks in the seamless logic of capitalism and patriarchy allow oppositional social practices and counterideologies to emerge.

Central to a materialist feminist analytic is its critical focus on ideology. Critique is a "decoding" practice that exposes textual boundaries and the ideologies that manage them, revealing the taken-for-granted order they perpetuate and opening up possibilities for change. Materialist feminism, then, situates these ideologies historically and materially and offers both a critical understanding of the object of inquiry as well as insights into how to effect emancipatory social change.

Conclusion

In the following chapters, these issues will be examined in relation to the heterosexual imaginary. Chapter 2, "The Wedding-Industrial Complex," illustrates the connections among major institutions involved or invested in the production of weddings and wedding ideology and discusses the significance of this complex. This chapter provides an examination of the wedding industry by making visible the commodification, accumulation, and labor issues underlying the consumption of the American white wedding. In addition to the primary wedding market, this chapter also identifies and discusses the secondary and tertiary markets in the wedding-industrial complex. Special attention is given to wedding gown marketing and production, wedding gifts, diamond rings, bridal magazines, honeymoons, children's toys and films, and the business of popular culture in relation to the wedding industry. This explanation of market forces is set in the context of "who marries" and explicates the material conditions upon which the wedding-industrial complex depends.

Chapter 3, "Romancing the Clone: The *White* Wedding," provides a close-up look at the bridal market, including an examination of bridal magazines, children's toys, celebrity wedding magazines, and the "Sunday Styles" section and wedding pages in the *Sunday New York Times*. This chapter explores the ways in which the heterosexual imaginary and its ideology of romantic love secure gender, race, class, and sexuality hierarchies; consent to the institution of heterosexuality; reproduce the division of labor; and control the accumulation of property.

Chapter 4, "Four Weddings and an Industry: Popular Film and Television Weddings," provides a critical reading of feature-length motion pictures, television weddings, and television advertising with wedding content. These are analyzed for the ways they participate in the production of the heterosexual imaginary through the patterns they reveal, the interests and consequences they obscure, and the ways they regulate gender, sexuality, race, and class.

The last chapter, "And They Lived Happily Ever After . . . " summarizes the findings of this study and offers recommendations for further research. The conclusion of this study, concerning the ways institutionalized heterosexuality has worked historically as a central form of capitalist and patriarchal social control, is elaborated. In particular, the ways the heterosexual imaginary underlies the romance with American weddings is highly consequential for gender, race, class, and sexuality and provides a model for whiteness in American culture. Particular attention is paid in this chapter to a discussion of the gay/lesbian marriage debates and to the new field of critical heterosexual studies.

Whenever a study seeks to intervene in the taken-for-granted and relations of ruling, it may create significant discomfort for those who benefit from these arrangements. *Allow yourself to be conscious of your reactions to this study.* Keep track of the moments when you experience the greatest resistance. These will provide you with evidence concerning the interests weddings serve in popular culture and to the ways each of us participates in the heterosexual imaginary.

What follows is one of the first in-depth examinations of weddings in American culture. As I've shared this project with numerous people over the past six years,

I've heard more wedding stories than it's possible to record. The depth of the heterosexual imaginary is sizable, and the consequences of romanticizing such seemingly benign and "fun-loving" practices are significant. What the white wedding keeps in place is nothing short of a racist, classist, and heterosexist social order. Is that what you planned for your wedding day?

At East High Elementary School in Mrs. Dolan's afternoon kindergarten class, Matthew and Melinda portrayed the letters Q and U during a wedding ceremony to teach kindergarteners that the letters are meant to be together. The wedding was complete with programs that read "Today I will marry my friend," the wedding march, and white wedding cake. The bride and groom exchanged candy rings. A disc jockey played the Carpenter's song "We've Only Just Begun." It was a lesson to show that the letters Q and U are always together in words.

"East High Kindergarteners Celebrate Special 'Wedding': Mr. Q and Miss U Joined in Ceremony" *Elizabethtown Chronicle*, v. 129, 1, 10/23–29/1997

Chapter Two

The Wedding-Industrial Complex

ecently referred to by Wall Street analysts as "recession-proof," the wedding
industry has reached such proportions that it can be more accurately described as
a wedding-industrial complex. This structure reflects the close association among
weddings, the transnational wedding industry, marriage, the state, religion, media,
and popular culture. To understand the significance of white weddings, it is crucial to attain a sense of the operation of the wedding industry particularly in relation to the workings of the wedding-industrial complex. The scope of this chapter
is to provide an overview of the various components of this complex in order to
make visible the historical and material foundation upon which the operation of
the heterosexual imaginary depends. Greater elaboration of the role of mass media
and popular culture and other aspects of the accompanying wedding-*ideological*
complex will be covered in subsequent chapters.

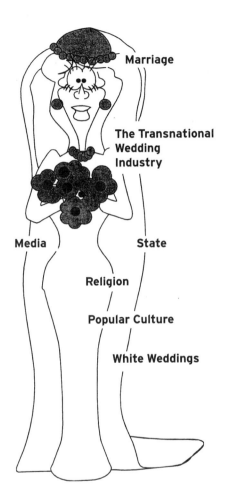

Marriage

The Transnational Wedding Industry

Media

State

Religion

Popular Culture

White Weddings

Table 2.1
The $32 billion
wedding industrial
complex

Marriage is a personal milestone and a consumer turning point. By age 35, the vast majority of Americans have been married at least once. Beyond the boost to industries related to the ceremony and honeymoon, marriage has a significant effect on the housing market, durable goods and financial services, to name a few.

—Bryant Robey, "Wedding-Bell Blues Chime as Marriage Markets Shift," *Adweek's Marketing Week*, June 25, 1990

The Transnational Wedding Industry

As of 1997, the *primary* wedding market in the United States represented total revenues of $32 billion. To put this in perspective, consider this: If these revenues were the product of one company, it would place in the top 25 *Fortune* 500 corporations. This multibillion-dollar industry includes the sale of a diverse range of products, many of which are produced outside of the U.S.—weddings gowns, dia-

Annual Revenues of $32 Billion Wedding Industry–1996

Table 2.2
Bride's 1997
Millennium Report:
Love & Money

Wedding apparel, invitations, flowers, reception, photos, gifts	$16.4 billion (51.3%)
Engagement/wedding rings	$ 3.3 billion (10.3%)
Honeymoon travel and apparel	$ 4.5 billion (14.1%)
Home furnishing, household equipment	$ 7.8 billion (24.3%)
	Total $32.0 Billion

monds, honeymoon travel and apparel, and household equipment. Also included in the market are invitations, flowers, receptions, photos, gifts, home furnishings, wedding cakes, catering, alcohol, paper products, calligraphy, jewelry, party supplies, hair styling, makeup, manicures, music, books, and wedding accessories, e.g., ring pillows, silver, chauffeurs, and limousines (*Bride's* 1997; *Modern Bride* 1994; Fields and Fields 1997). (See Table 2.2 and the Appendix for company listings.)[1] Although newlyweds make up only 2.6 percent of all American households, "they account for 75% of all the fine china, 29% of the tableware, and 21% of the jewelry and watches sold in this country every year" (Dogar 1997). Even insurers have entered the primary wedding market by offering coverage to cover the cost of any monies already spent on the wedding preparation "if wedding bells don't ring." Fireman's Fund Insurance Company offers "Weddingsurance" for wedding catastrophes such as flood or fire (but not for "change of heart") (Haggerty 1993). In fact, attach the words wedding or bridal to nearly any item and its price goes up. With June as the leading wedding month, followed by August and July, summer becomes a wedding marketer's dream.

According to industry estimates, the average wedding in the United States costs $19,104, with some regional variations. For instance, in the New York metro area the average wedding increases to $29,454. In the Midwest, the cost drops to $16,195 and on the West Coast, $18,918 (*Bride's* 1997). Considered in relation to what Americans earn, the cost of the average wedding represents 51 percent of the mean earnings of a white family of four and 89 percent of the median earnings for black[2] families. The fact that 63.7 percent of Americans earn less than $25,000 per year (U.S. Bureau of the Census 1996) means the average cost of a wedding approximates a year's earnings for many Americans. It costs less to pay the average price for a year in college—$17,823 (College Board 1997)—and about the same to purchase a new Honda Accord or Ford Taurus (Wright 1999).

The Wedding Debt

The level of debt incurred by newlyweds has received some media attention but with little effect on wedding consumption patterns. One article in the *Boston Globe* in 1996 referred to the newlywed experience with the wedding industry as "wedding hell" (With 1996). The article described a fairly typical encounter with the wedding industry. Working against classic arguments such as "It's the happiest day of your life" and "It's a once-in-a-lifetime thing," the newlyweds in this article struggled to plan a wedding that would not exceed $5,000. What they found shocked them. After weeks of bartering with reception halls and caterers who were either unwilling to negotiate or were priced out of reach, the bride said, "I was exhausted. Planning a wedding is a full-time job, a second one for me—and not even as rewarding. My fiancé and I were feeling like the victims of highway robbers with sanctioned routines" (With 1996, 85:1). The final blow was attending a crowded bridal show where they had to "register" for numerous mailing lists and the bride was given a "silly sticker," which proclaimed her "a very important bride," and told to fill out fifty-eight coupons for special prizes. "These people must think *bride* is synonymous with *stupid,*" she thought. In the end, this couple decided not to get married yet and instead to put their $5,000 toward the purchase of a house, where, in the end, they could hold their own wedding and reception.

Another couple, having seen the corruption and greed of the wedding industry, decided to become consumer advocates. Denise and Alan Fields, authors of *Bridal Bargains* (1997) and *Bridal Gown Guide* (1998), have nearly single-handedly taken on the unregulated wedding industry. With statements such as "too many wedding businesses have the morals of an average slug" (1998a), the Fieldses have turned their negative experience in planning their own wedding into advocacy in the interests of newlyweds. In so doing, they have encountered the wrath of some

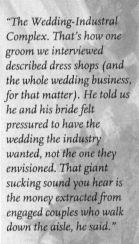

"The Wedding-Industrial Complex. That's how one groom we interviewed described dress shops (and the whole wedding business, for that matter). He told us he and his bride felt pressured to have the wedding the industry wanted, not the one they envisioned. That giant sucking sound you hear is the money extracted from engaged couples who walk down the aisle, he said."

Bridal Gown Guide, 29

wedding businesses attempting to preserve their questionable, and in some cases illegal, practices. We'll return to this later in this chapter.

Who Are the Targets of the Wedding Industry?

Who marries, and who are the consumers of this enormous industry? On average, newlyweds are getting older. As of March 1997, the Census Bureau reported that the mean age for brides has risen to 25 and for grooms, 26.8 years. The age of first marriage has been rising steadily at a rate of one year every decade for first marriages. Social acceptance of couples living together prior to marriage, higher education, and career opportunities are contributing to these increases, which also change the marketing of weddings. Many young couples now own houses and many of the home furnishings they need before they marry. The effect is a shift in marketing strategy that opens up the wedding gift market to include everything from tools to lawnmowers to sports equipment.

The total number of marriages and remarriages in 1996 was 2,342,000, which represents 2 percent of the total U.S. age-fifteen-and-over population (*Bride's* 1996; U.S. Bureau of the Census 1996). This rate—of 8.8 per 1,000 persons—has remained relatively stable since 1990, when the number of marriages reached an all-time high of 2,448,000. Quite a considerable marketing niche!

Contributing to the health of the wedding industry, the remarriage market is large and complex and "includes some married people who want to reaffirm their vows in second ceremonies" (Dewitt 1992).[3] With the current divorce rate at 4.6 per 1,000 persons, about 46 percent of annual marriages are remarriages for at least one member of the couple. The average age for the divorced woman who remarries is 35, and the average for divorced men is 39. Even though remarriage weddings tend to be smaller, the wedding industry estimates they total up to 30 percent of their revenues, which shows that at least one sector in American society actually benefits from divorce. In fact, without remarriages, the wedding industry would be substantially smaller.

According to the wedding industry, today's newlyweds are also more likely to be dual-earner couples, with 83 percent of brides and 89 percent of grooms working; they earn a combined income currently twice that of the average household, at $65,076 (*Bride's* 1995/1996, Bridal Market Acquisition Report). Factoring in the age and financial standing of many of those remarrying, the probability of higher incomes increases, as does the focus of the wedding market on the consumption patterns of these newlyweds.

Fascinating, right? But there's something missing from this picture of the wedding market. In researching data on the wedding industry and its markets, one striking pattern emerges. Almost without exception, most state and industry analysts have overlooked the effects of race and class on consumption. For the most part, the data collected concerning wedding and marriage patterns focus primarily on middle-class whites. When recalculated to account for differences along racial, ethnic, and class lines, these figures change dramatically. For example, the average black couple spends an average of $10,000 on a wedding, significantly less than the average $19,104 mentioned in most research. The 88 percent marriage rate for Americans cited in wedding industry and census materials is primarily applicable to whites and is significantly lower for hispanics (68 percent) and even lower yet for blacks (46 percent). While blacks used to marry much younger, they now marry considerably later than the national average. Twenty-five percent of black women and less than 12 percent of black men have married by their early twenties, and more than 43.4 percent of blacks have never married, compared to 23.8 percent of whites. These numbers get even more dramatic when you break them down by sex (see Table 2.3).

What is significant about this data is the impact these patterns have on the wedding industry. Wedding marketers are aware that white middle-class women are more likely to consume wedding products than any other group, and so they target their marketing campaigns to white women.

Table 2.3
Black and White
Never Married Rates.
Source: U.S. Dept of
Commerce and the
Census Bureau 1994

NEVER MARRIED	WOMEN	MEN
Black	40.3%	47.1%
White	20.2%	27.6%

The average combined income for marrieds from "other" groups is also significantly lower, given the disproportionate representation of blacks and hispanics in lower income brackets. For instance, 33.1 percent of blacks have earnings below the national poverty threshold as compared with 14.5 percent of the entire U.S. population.[4] Even though blacks achieve parity with whites in elementary and secondary education, only 12.9 percent complete four or more years of college as compared with the national average of 22.2 percent (U.S. Bureau of the Census 1996). Given the relationship of education to earning potential, the combined earnings of black or hispanic newlyweds are usually significantly lower than those of whites and are likely to remain lower throughout the course of the marriage (which is also shorter).

Why are there differences in marriage rates between whites, blacks, and hispanics? In attempting to answer this question, especially in relation to the high percentage of single mothers—blacks, 48 percent, hispanics, 25 percent, and whites, 14 percent—researchers have identified the problem of the "marriage penalty" (Besharov and Sullivan 1996; Steurle 1995). Marriages among the middle class generally increase the earning potential of individuals. Certainly, for middle- to upper-class white women, marriage means financial security. The rewards and benefits afforded these couples and their families—from health insurance to health club discounts—even though married persons incur a marriage tax penalty—are substantial.

However, among those earning minimum wage or living near or below the poverty line, marriage disqualifies many for the benefits they need to survive. The risk is that even a working husband's earnings may be "too much" for him to qualify for a host of programs including food stamps, school meals, and child care but not enough to lift the family out of poverty. As the 1997 census data indicate, an increasing number of couples are choosing to live together without "benefit" of marriage in order to avoid losing these programs, Social Security income, and some tax breaks. Ultimately, then, marriage only privileges those who already have the earnings to stay out of poverty. This means *marriage primarily benefits groups that are not disproportionately represented among the poor and that are able to secure and maintain goods and property.* Clearly, to blame the loss of "family values" as the "problem" with the poor is a myth! It is a myth that deceives the public, distorts the issues, and blames the victims.

The Future Market

Two factors of particular significance that may influence wedding marketers in the future have to do with new reports on "black consumption" patterns. In a study released in July 1998, economist Jeffrey Humphreys reported that black spending power is growing faster than the national average. The study forecasts that black consumers will "account for 8.2 percent of total buying power in 1999, compared with 7.4 percent in 1990" (Sewell 1998, C2). The other factor that may affect wedding marketers is the increase in the black population, which is also growing faster than the U.S. population as a whole, at 14 percent versus 9 percent. Humphreys credited these gains to economic expansion and educational progress made by blacks in recent years.

One of the key problems with Humphreys's study is history. These numbers reflect the gains made in education and economics in the past and do not show the effects of recent rollbacks in affirmative action, which are decreasing black enrollments in higher education. While gains have been made, black men still earn only 72 cents for every dollar white men make, and black women earn 85 cents for every dollar white women are paid. If these disparities continue, "white" weddings will persist as sites to exemplify and perpetuate racial hierarchies.

Wedding marketers are aware of these facts as well. They know that income patterns among whites promise greater return on their investment. As you will see in the next chapter, bridal magazines are notorious for overlooking women of color in their advertisements and marketing of weddings. The overriding effect of these patterns is that in terms of affordability and necessity, the wedding in American culture is primarily a ritual by, for, and about the white middle to upper classes. Truly, the *white* wedding.

The primary wedding market depends on numerous production and labor relations issues that underlie the consumption and accumulation involved in weddings. The central purpose of including them here is to make visible the historical

and material conditions that set the conditions for the production of the white wedding. While gown marketing is probably the most insidious, other wedding products and services also warrant coverage here. To examine each area of the primary wedding market falls outside the scope of this book. The following section offers highlights of the primary wedding market in the form of case studies.

Primary Wedding Market
Background: White Wedding Gowns

Probably the most significant wedding purchase is the wedding gown. Industry analysts have noted that most brides would do without many things to plan a wedding and stay within budget, but they would not scrimp when it comes to the purchase of the wedding gown. With the national average expenditure at $823 for the gown and $199 for the veil, the bride's apparel becomes the centerpiece of the white wedding. Most of us have heard the various phrases associated with the bride and her gown, the symbolic significance attached to how she looks and how beautiful her gown is. In coverage of Barbra Streisand's wedding in *People* magazine, the bulk of the photos are of her in a white "shimmering crystal-beaded Donna Karan gown with a 15-foot diaphanous veil" (July 20, 1998). This reference, as well as those of many other celebrities, imitates the standard-bearers of fame, privilege, style, and perfection: Queen Victoria, Queen Elizabeth, Princess Grace, and Princess Diana.

Prior to Queen Victoria (1819–1901), white wedding gowns were not the norm. Brides wore brocades of golds and silvers, yellows and blues. Puritan women wore gray. But Victoria's wedding in February 1840 captured the imaginations of many when this powerful presider over the British empire, who many thought of as "plain," married a handsome man. She did so in an opulent ceremony where she wore a luxurious and beautiful (by nineteenth-century standards) *white* wedding gown. Following this grand event, many white Western middle-class brides imitated Victoria and adopted the white wedding gown. By the turn of the century, white had not only become the standard but had also become laden with symbolism—it stood for purity, virginity, innocence, and promise, as well as power and privilege.

"As a young woman in Anne Tyler's latest novel, Ladder of Years, *asks her father in all seriousness on the eve of her wedding, 'Which is more trouble: calling off the wedding or suing for divorce?'"*

—Bernard 1995

Princess Grace

Queen Elizabeth II's wedding to Prince Philip in 1947 once again seized the attention of people around the world. This post-World War II extravaganza was not only a wedding of royalty and affluence, but it came at a time following the devastation and gloom of the war when many Westerners were desperately seeking images of hope, prosperity, and order. For years to come, these two major public spectacles secured the promise of, and romance with, the white wedding so prevalent today.

Continuing this powerful tradition in recent years were the weddings of two pre-eminent princess brides: Princess Grace and Princess Diana. These blond-haired, blue-eyed, real-life princess Barbies married during the mass media era. The former Grace Kelly (1929–1982) was a beautiful, famous, internationally acclaimed film star who met a handsome prince, Prince Rainier of Monaco, married in April 1956, and went off to live "happily ever after" as Princess Grace of Monaco. For many Americans, Grace Kelly, born in Philadelphia to Irish immigrant parents, represented the merging of the Hollywood fairy-tale happy ending and the American dream of possibility and wealth. The headlines proclaimed that even a little girl from Philadelphia could become a princess.

Lady Diana Spencer, previously unknown to the public, married one of the most affluent, famous, and eligible bachelors of the late twentieth century, Prince Charles. Also blond, blue-eyed, and beautiful, the nineteen-year-old Lady Diana became the wife of the future king of England. Their wedding was a globally televised public spectacle watched by 750 million people from all parts of the world. In both weddings the brides wore extraordinarily elaborate and expensive white wedding gowns and were married in ceremonies befitting a queen—extravagant, luxurious, and opulent. Here's how *People* magazine described Diana's wedding:

> The euphoria was overwhelming, the images unforgettable. Perfect!
> proclaimed London's **Daily Mail** in the banner headline over its front-
> page photo of the kissing newlyweds. The Very Picture of Fairy-Tale
> Sweethearts, echoed the **Sun.** It was July 29, 1981, the wedding of His
> Royal Highness, the Prince of Wales and Lady Diana Spencer, seemingly
> destined to become King and Queen of England. . . . It was all spectacle
> and wonderment and celebration, not a day of doubt. (**People** 1991, 23)

These modern-day fairy tales captured the imagination of many—women and men, young and old, lesbian and gay. These women's lives symbolized possibility: "Fairy tales can come true, it can happen to you." Neither woman came from royalty—Grace was a movie star and Diana was a kindergarten teacher born of nobility—yet both found "a handsome prince," leading many to believe that fairy tales

Princess Diana

could come true. Both women became fetishized by fans, who followed and studied their every move. Both women became tragic figures to their adoring public when they each died at young ages in spectacular car crashes.

Of course, the notion of the fantasy marriage the fairy tale promised was shattered when revelations of Diana's and Prince Charles's extramarital affairs were made public and their marriage ended in divorce. Still, Diana's funeral was one of the most watched events in television history. Her death, her failed happily-ever-after life, is considered by many to be one of the greatest tragedies in modern times. During the televising of the events surrounding her death, all networks replayed scenes from her wedding to Charles. Newscasters repeatedly referred to her wedding, replaying images of Diana and Charles on the balcony of Buckingham Castle, their ride through the streets of London in the royal, horsedrawn carriage, the view of her entering Westminster Abbey in her extraordinary white wedding gown:

> London, July 29—For her long walk up the aisle that transformed her into a princess, Lady Diana Spencer, in the most romantic storybook tradition, wore a sequin-and-pearl-incrusted dress with a 25-foot train. Made of ivory silk taffeta produced by Britain's only silk farm the dress was hand-embroidered with old lace panels on the front and back of the tightly fitting boned bodice. A wide frill edged the scooped neckline, and the loose, full sleeves were caught at the elbow with taffeta bows. A multi-layered tulle crinoline propped up the diaphanous skirt.
>
> A diamond tiara belonging to Earl Spencer, Lady Diana's father, anchored her ivory tulle veil, aglitter with thousands of hand-sewn sequins. Also borrowed was a pair of diamond drop earrings from Lady Diana's mother. . . . For the final tradition-bound item—something blue—a blue bow was sewn into the waistband of the dress. A fiercely and successfully kept secret, the dress had been guarded day and night by a security organization at the workrooms of the designers, David and Elizabeth Emanuel. (Anderson 1981, p. 1)

Diana's wedding and gown have had a profound influence on the wedding industry. Nearly every aspect of her wedding has been detailed time and again on television and in bridal and news magazines. The wedding of Diana and Charles became the exemplar of the ultimate fantasy of what a wedding should be:

> The union of Lady Diana Spencer and Charles, Prince of Wales, transformed the way we think about weddings. The images of that event are so thoroughly implanted in our memories, it's hard to separate the

idea of a bride from the picture of Diana emerging, Cinderella-like, from
her glass coach. That early morning . . . we started dreaming about the
day when we, too, would promise to love, honor, and cherish. (**Bride's**
1997/1998, 40)

Wedding advertising reflects these images in varying forms over and over again.
Consider this quote from the August/September 1998 issue of *Bride's* magazine:

What makes a woman obsess about her wedding gown? Is it because
she's been thinking about it since she was four, because it's the one item
of clothing that can instantly turn her into a princess, or because 167
pairs of eyes will be staring at her as she marches down the aisle? Write
The Great White Hope, **Bride's** Magazine, 140 E. 45th Street, New York,
NY 10017. (6)

Not only does this paragraph invite the reader (bride) to imagine herself as bride,
princess, and spectacle, but it naturalizes this desire by suggesting she's had this
dream since she was four. In fact, this fantasy is the work of both the wedding-
industrial and the wedding-ideological complexes. The play on words characterized by the phrase "the great white hope," a slogan emanating from a battle
between a white boxer and a black boxer, offers a troubling association between
the desire for the white wedding and racism. (As you will see in the following discussion of the wedding industry and in Chapter 3, this "great white hope" goes far
beyond the white wedding gown.)

The marketing of everything from weddings to gowns to children's toys to popular wedding films to Disney is laced with messages about fairy tales and princesses. Even couture fashion shows of world-class designers traditionally feature wedding gowns as their grand finale. As I will show, it is this romance with the white
wedding gown and the fantasy bride that conceals the workings of the heterosexual imaginary throughout the wedding-industrial complex. Moreover, the inter-
dependency of weddings with the historical needs of capitalism becomes virtually invisible. The wedding gown becomes fetishized, creating a "recession-proof"

market where social relations become alienated in favor of the pursuit of the ultimate commodity—the couture or couture-like wedding gown.

Purchasing the Wedding Gown

The vast majority of bridal stores are specialty shops that cater to the bride with all sorts of distinctive treatment. These stores are the mainstay of a very well-established and lucrative bridal gown industry. In addition to the cost of the gown and

Fairy-tale wedding
gown from Mary's
Bridal of P. C.
Mary's, Inc.

veil, brides spend hundreds of dollars accessorizing with lingerie, shoes, and jewelry.

The only ripple in this well-established wedding gown business has been created by the entry of David's Bridal, formerly David's Bridal Warehouse, a chain of sixty off-the-rack superstores, and Discount Bridal Service (DBS). What had formerly been a secure and expensive bridal gown market has become pressured by discount stores offering up to two thousand dresses in sizes 4 to 26 with prices ranging from $200 to $1,000, with no special orders and no waiting. The bridal gown industry, threatened by the discount gown stores, is generally hostile toward

Wedding gown in
bridal store

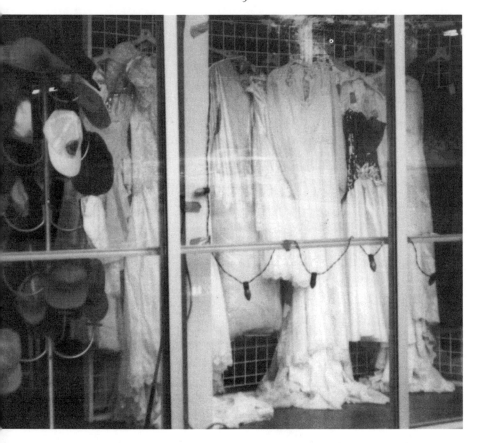

Wedding gowns in
thrift store window

the discount market, primarily because, as the Fieldses argue in *Bridal Gown Guide*, the "Discount Bridal Service is the bride's secret weapon in the war on high prices" (Fields 1998, 53). With brides as a "captive" audience, the wedding industry has—and wants to hold on to—their marketing edge. Even the publisher of *Vows* was reluctant to share his industry trade journal with anyone outside the industry for fear it would provide customers with too much inside information.

Filene's, aware of the demand for discounted bridal gowns, opens their basement doors four times a year to would-be brides seeking to purchase couture dresses at bargain basement prices. Customers begin lining up at 5:00 a.m. and rush

Bridal gown store
out of business

the racks when the store opens. Within a matter of minutes, all the dresses are off the racks and women are trying them on in the aisles. When someone finds the gown she wants the crowd applauds and rush her remaining gowns. Clearly, these sales combined with the increasing presence of discount bridal stores represent an interruption in business-as-usual for gown retailers.

But specialty gown stores are not all they appear to be. One practice gown stores use is telling the bride they don't have her size or that she is larger than she thought (always fun to hear!); this results in a special order or the purchase of a dress that is too large and requires alterations. Of course, those alterations are done in the store for costs of $80 to $250 by seamstresses frequently working for substandard wages.

Another practice widely engaged in by gown-sellers is the removal of designer labels and prices from dresses. In many surveys, from *Modern Bride* to Dawn Currie's interview study (1993), brides indicate that they rely upon bridal magazines to give them ideas about what type of gown to choose. They take the ad for the gown they like best to area stores and attempt to try on and purchase that particular dress. What they encounter is a system of deception widely practiced by many bridal shops. First, sellers remove the labels. Brides ask for a Vera Wang or an Alfred Angelo or a Jessica McClintock and are told to get the number off the gown so the clerk can check their book and see which designer it is. The bride has no way of knowing if she actually has the brand she seeks. As I toured various shops and saw how widespread this practice was, I asked store owners why they removed the labels from the dresses. Without exception they told me that it was to maintain the integrity of their business and to prevent women from comparison shopping. The truth is, this practice is *illegal* and provides shop owners with a great deal of flexibility in preserving their customer base and profit margin. Alan and Denise Fields have documented many of these practices in their *Bridal Gown Guide*, providing brides with important consumer information:

> By our estimates, three out of four shops intentionally remove tags out of their dresses. Why? They want to keep you dumb. If you knew who made which dress, you could go down the street to that evil Debbie Does Discount Bridal Gown Shoppe and get it at a 25% discount. All this would be fine if it weren't illegal. Yes, there is a federal law that outlaws this practice. The Federal Textile Products Identification Act, Title 15, Sec 70 . . . says all apparel sold in this country must include a label with the manufacturer's name, the fiber content and the country of origin. . . . The law was enacted in 1958. (1998, 33)

In addition to this federal consumer protection law, many states provide similar protections. But bridal gown stores have little to fear: this law is not enforced. And, perhaps more importantly, the romance with the white wedding gown distracts the soon-to-be brides from becoming suspicious of store practices.

Wedding Gown Production

If you look at the portion of tags gown-sellers leave in the dresses you will see that most are sewn outside the U.S. in countries such as Guatemala, Mexico, Taiwan, and China. Nearly 80 percent of all wedding gowns are produced outside the U.S. in subcontracted factories where labor standards are nowhere near what they are in the U.S. and no unions or regulators keep watch. Elson and Pearson quote from an investment brochure designed to attract multinational corporations:

> The manual dexterity of the oriental female is famous the world over. Her hand are small and she works fast with extreme care. Who, therefore, could be better qualified by **nature and inheritance** to contribute to the efficiency of a bench-assembly production line than the oriental girl? (1981, p. 93).

The recruitment of U.S. companies to contract offshore labor benefits manufacturers on many levels: cheap labor, low overhead, fewer regulations, and higher profits. And with the proliferation of free trade agreements such as the North Atlantic Free Trade Agreement (NAFTA) and the General Agreement on Tarriffs and Trade (GATT), labor and environmental abuses abound. Particularly in locations such as the free trade zone in Mexico where proximity to the U.S. and eco-

From *Bridal Gown Guide* E-Mail:

"After several weeks of gown shopping, I have learned that this experience is not for the faint of heart or the uninformed. . . . I was not about to plunk down 60% deposit only to find out that the dress was made by a no-name company in a sweatshop in China" (1998, 6).

```
SIZE ___18___

COLOR _Eggplant_

          CONTENTS
SHELL  - 100% POLYESTER
LINING - 100% POLYESTER

DO NOT WASH OR SPOT CLEAN.
DRY CLEAN ONLY, BY USING
  THE ZURCION METHOD.
    WE RECOMMEND
CONTINENTAL DRY CLEANERS.
   1-800-242-GOWN.
FREE PICK-UP NATIONWIDE.
GUARANTEED PROCESSING.

    STEAM ON
REVERSE SIDE ONLY

     RN# 85449
  MADE IN MEXICO
```

Bridesmaid gown tag

nomic relations between the U.S. government and Mexico make this a largely unregulated location, occupational hazards, toxic exposure and dumping, sexual harassment, and labor abuses yield significant increases in profits for manufacturers and produce immeasurable costs to the people and lands in these areas.

With the exception of Jessica McClintock's dresses, most are made offshore. But even McClintock's labor practices in the U.S. have come under scrutiny. While her firm joined the 1996 Fashion Trendsetters List of the U.S. Department of Labor pledging to "help eradicate sweatshops in America" (Ross 1997), McClintock's own textile workers in the U.S. went unpaid when her subcontractor filed bankruptcy (Cacas 1994).

In 1996, then Secretary of Labor Robert Reich gathered industry leaders together to head off a labor and offshore manufacturing crisis precipitated by the National Labor Committee's (NLC) exposure of sweatshop use by The Gap and by Wal-Mart's Kathie Lee Gifford clothing line. In a press release that coincided with the holiday season and the anniversary of the Triangle Shirtwaist Factory fire in New York City in 1909, in which 145 women died as a result of sweatshop working conditions, Reich released a "no sweat" initiative in the form of a Trendsetter's List. This directory of garment manufacturers and retailers provided consumers with a list of companies committed to taking "additional steps to ensure their goods are not made in sweatshop conditions" (U.S. Department of Labor 1996). While the list was extensive, the only wedding gown manufacturer in evidence was designer Jessica McClintock.

The Asian Immigrant Women's Association (AIWA) launched a full-scale campaign to force McClintock to pay her workers $10,000 in back wages. When they saw McClintock's name on the Trendsetters' List they contacted the Labor Department and threatened to expose the company for labor abuses. Rather than risk media exposure, McClintock settled with the workers over the back pay they were owed (Cacas 1994).

With the exception of an investigation into labor abuses on the part of one leading dress manufacturer by the Union of Needletrades, Industrial and Textile Employees (UNITE), little is being done by designers or governments to ensure legal and humane treatment of wedding apparel textile workers. Compared to

In July 1998, United Steelworkers of America, AFL-CIO-CLC, et. al. filed a federal lawsuit questioning the constitutionality of NAFTA. "The so-called free trade system that NAFTA established . . . has given predatory corporations a license to hunt for the cheapest labor and the lowest environmental and safety standards on the continent."

—George Becker,
Coalition for Justice
in the Maquiladoras
530 Bandera Road
San Antonio, Texas 78228

major corporations such as Nike, Mattel, and Wal-Mart, most of these smaller textile operations are overlooked and unexamined.

Lifting the Veil: A Special Report, a white paper distributed by UNITE in 1997, documents the sweatshop practices of the Alfred Angelo Company (Sailer 1997). Alfred Angelo, a Philadelphia-based gown manufacturer founded by the Piccione family in 1940, has had a long-standing reputation in the design and production of wedding and prom gowns and bridesmaid and mother-of-the-bride dresses. Under labels such as Christian Dior, Michele Piccione Couture, Tina Michele, Dance-Allure, Flirtations, Bridallure, and Alfred Angelo Bridals, the company has sold gowns and dresses through the J.C. Penney bridal catalog as well as through retail sales.

In a survey conducted by UNITE in April 1997 of three factories in Guatemala, it was discovered that Alfred Angelo gowns were being made by thirteen-year-olds in factories with widespread violations of their country's child labor, wage, and hour laws and under life-threatening safety conditions. At two of the firms, four-teen- and fifteen-year-olds worked as long as ten hours a day earning $20.80 a week.

Even though sales volumes have risen steadily, according to UNITE, Alfred Angelo plans to eliminate jobs in the United States and move all of its work to Guatemala. With annual sales at $59 million in 1996, the company still seeks to use Chinese subcontractors to assemble dresses. UNITE reports that "there is no way of knowing the conditions under which the clothes are made" and that Alfred Angelo's primary motivation is "greed." Angelo laborers in the U.S. have "allied themselves with the exploited workers in Guatemala and China" in an effort to convince the Piccione family to put corporate responsibility ahead of corporate greed.

In June 1997 the Alfred Angelo Company apologized for late deliveries and cited union trouble as the reason. They blamed the problems on "militant and negative responses from UNITE apparel union, which has directly contributed to the delay of shipments to our customers" (Fields 1997). A sagging bridal retail market has recently contributed to sales declines, and companies like Alfred Angelo have been pressured by discount bridal retailers who "undercut their prices on gowns," as

"Every bride sees her wedding day as the culmination of her dreams, and every wedding is a celebration of that," believes *[Michele] Piccione. "Sure, styles change, but the sense of fantasy is always there. And as the largest bridalwear manufacturer in the country, we try to meet every fantasy that's out there."*

Quote by the chief designer and daughter of founders of the Piccione-owned and -operated gown manufacturer, Alfred Angelo (Friedman 1997).

Sweatshop photos
from UNITE

UNITE workers
protest against
wedding dress
manufacturer
Alfred Angelo
at a June 1997
rally in
Philadelphia.
Photos
courtesy of
UNITE

well as by "rising couture stars like Amsale" (Fields 1997). In this spring's bridal fashion review in New York, Alfred Angelo was conspicuously absent, leaving many with the impression that the company is having difficulty recovering from these setbacks.

Another boon for the gown industry is the growing appeal of the white Western wedding gown in many locations around the globe, for example in Japan, South Asia, and parts of Africa. The influence of global capitalism and the transnational wedding industry can be felt in many countries in the use of laborers and in the supplanting of culturally specific traditions with markers of the dominant, such as the very symbolic white wedding gown.

Wedding Gifts

More than $18 billion a year is spent on gifts for the bride and groom (*Modern Bride* 1994). Advice abounds in the wedding literature on how much to spend, where to buy, and, most importantly, what to buy for newlyweds. One recent article in *Ladies' Home Journal* advised wedding-goers that "the price of the gift should at least cover the cost of your place at the reception and should reflect your relationship with the couple" (Rosen 1995, 100).

Bridal magazines feature an enormous range of possibilities for newlyweds to consider. Bridal registries in most businesses from china to hardware are now available, so the bride and groom can accumulate a variety of goods for their lives together. Department stores are devoting extra time to their registry services in the knowledge that bridal registry purchases can account for 50 percent of sales. In fact, registries have become so successful that some retailers are calling them "gift" registries instead of "bridal" ones, thereby capitalizing on the nonwedding market as well. Crate and Barrel, which sells everything from bathmats to sofas, shifted from the name "bridal" to "gift" to make themselves more accessible to a broader range of consumers. "We now list people as registrant and co-registrant instead of bride and groom, which makes everyone comfortable, including gay couples" (Hamlin 1996).

Most retailers acknowledge that the bridal industry is a growing business for them. Not only are the number of weddings considerable, but the current trend is

Call it a leap of faith. Call it traditionalism or romanticism—even masochism, as the maritally wounded might see it. Call it whatever you want but give it its due: the wedding season, like the baseball season that runs around the same time, is a season of boundless hope.

—Bob Levin, "Leap of Faith," *Maclean's*, June 28, 1993, pp. 34–42.

toward large up-scale weddings. The average wedding now includes about two hundred fifty people (*Bride's* 1997). To meet the needs of this growing market, retailers are now increasing staff to service guests who need assistance in choosing the right wedding gift. As a result they are noticing greater returns on their investment. With the age of the couple increasing, buying power also increases, as does the range of gift possibilities. The effect is that stores are expanding their registry listings to accommodate the couple's every whim (though of all the gifts couples are interested in, studies have shown the number one preference for 88 percent of those surveyed is cash [Hamlin 1996]).

Surveying the articles and magazines by, for, and about the wedding industry, it becomes evident that the level of expenditure expected of newlyweds and wedding-goers is primarily in the interest of creating a spectacle of luxury and status. In these periodicals, two themes resonate throughout but particularly in relation to gift purchases: that marriage increases the potential for consumption and accumulation.

In a recent article, "Wedlock Has Its Benefits" by Larry Strauss, the author advises Generation Xers of the many pluses of getting married: no more singles bars, no more "weird dates from hell," and someone to love you even when you're fat, ugly, and poorly behaved. But, Strauss says,

> [W]ho can forget quite possibly the coolest part: getting of gifts . . .
> proper planning on your part and a little creativity, your list-making can
> go a long way to aid wedded bliss. . . . [T]oday's young people generally
> wait much longer than their parents did to get married. Hence they've
> accumulated a lot of stuff. . . . [I]t pays to make your unique needs
> known to potential gift-givers. . . . In noting gifts you'd like, be sure to
> consider your hobbies and lifestyle. . . . [Y]ou have to be mindful of two
> basic tenets of tactful gift-requesting . . . varying price ranges to suit all
> budgets . . . [and] don't forget those thank-you cards. (1994)

What stands out in this piece is the emphasis on attaining goods from wedding-goers. For this author, anyway, the message is get somebody to marry you and you can be badly behaved and get what really counts: gifts! This advice is very conscious of the changing demographics and the benefits of getting married later—you can be more precise in what gifts you want, what interests these gifts will serve, and how to make sure gift-givers know what to buy.

Diamond Wedding Jewelry

As part of the fantasy of the ever-romantic marriage proposal, the diamond ring takes center stage. In fact, for 70 percent of all U.S. brides and 75 percent of first-time brides, the first purchase for the impending wedding is the diamond engagement ring. The central marketing strategy of the world's largest diamond-mining organization, De Beers, is to convince consumers that "diamonds are forever." Once you accept this slogan, you also believe that you're making a life-long investment, not just purchasing a bauble for your bride! In fact, De Beers spends about $57 million each year on this advertising campaign and has "committed to spending a large part of [their] budget—some $200 million this year—on the promotion of diamond jewelry around the world" (Oppenheimer 1998, 8). De Beers and its advertisers have developed a new "shadow" campaign to sell to consumers the advice that the "appropriate" diamond engagement ring should cost at least "two months' salary" for the groom (*Jewelers'* 1996). This advertising strategy signals to newlyweds—grooms in particular—that anything less is not acceptable. The diamond industry this has effectively convinced us that purchasing a diamond engagement ring is no longer a luxury but a necessity. Not surprisingly, according to wedding industry estimates, this message is reaching its target. The average expenditure for engagement rings is $3,000 (*Modern Bride* 1996). This figure translates into an annual salary of approximately $26,000 per year, the income bracket many of these ads target.

Diamonds, from the Greek *adamas*, for unconquerable, were discovered more than two thousand years ago in India and are believed to be the most enduring and hardest natural substance known to humankind. While their pyramid-like shapes and durability have evoked much mystery, it is the labor and technology required in the mining and processing that have had the most effect on the cost of these gems. According to the diamond industry, it takes the mining of 250 tons of earth

It was the handfasting, not the marriage ceremony, which produced the exchange of vows which are now part of the Anglican wedding service. And, it was the handfasting which produced the word "wed." This originally meant the pledge, the sum of money handed over to the girl's father. Later it also came to mean the ring which was given at the same time, and which was worn on the bride-to-be's right hand until the marriage. During the wedding ceremony, the groom transferred the "wed" to the bride's left hand, holding it in turn over the tips of the thumb and the first two finger and saying "in the name of the Father," for the thumb; "in the name of the Son" for the index finger; "in the name of the Holy Ghost," for the middle finger; and, finally, "Amen," as he slipped it into place on the third finger. . . . [H]aving been handed one of the bride's slippers by her father (to signify the transfer of authority), he bopped the bride smartly on the head with it (to signify that he was now her master). The weapon was later . . . placed over the bed—on the husband's side.

—Monsarrat 1973

to produce a one-carat polished diamond. From mining and processing to cutting and sales, a diamond touches at least five continents and involves the skills of many laborers before it is worn by the bride-to-be.

By the fifteenth century, diamond rings were a routine feature of the weddings of kings, queens, and other royalty. The rarity of these gems and the changes in cutting techniques—from styles that absorbed light to patterns that reflected light—made diamonds more beautiful, mysterious, highly prized, and available only to the elite.

The discovery of diamonds in Brazil in the eighteenth century increased their availability and appeal. In 1870 supply met with demand when great quantities of diamonds were discovered in Africa. With increased availability the prices of diamonds declined and the diamond engagement ring became more accessible to the lower classes. What Queen Victoria did for the white wedding gown, she also did for diamonds. Throughout the nineteenth century, she purchased an enormous collection of diamonds of all sizes and values, making them the gem of choice among the royalty-following masses. Her engagement ring was a "snake ring" with diamonds in the eyes of the snake.

By the twentieth century, messages about diamonds rings were popularized. In the film *Gentlemen Prefer Blondes* a famous phrase about the role of diamonds in a woman's life emerged: "Men grow cold as girls grow old, and we lose all our charms in the end. . . . But square-cut or pear-shape, these rocks don't lose their shape, diamonds are a girl's best friend" (American Gem Society 1998). This famous passage helped to make the diamond engagement ring the ultimate symbol of lasting heterosexual love. Even when we are too old to be passionate or beautiful, the diamond will still radiate. This gem will serve as a beacon of light, ever reminding the romantic of what was once bright and beautiful.

In addition to the purchase of an engagement ring, newlyweds have also been convinced they *must* buy wedding rings—at an average cost of $1,159 (Schoolman 1997). Nearly 100 percent of brides receive a wedding band. Grooms, on the other hand, have not historically been required to wear a ring. The "betrothal ring" traditionally signified the pledge that the marriage contract guaranteeing the trans-

"Centuries ago, grooms presented rings as partial payment for the bride"

—Lee 1994, p. 35

fer of a woman as property from the father to the groom would be honored. This ancient Roman tradition was adopted by the Christians early in the first century and became an integral part of the church ceremony. Currently, the trend in the U.S. is toward the groom also wearing a wedding band, usually made of gold. Today, 90 percent of grooms receive a wedding ring, and 20 percent wear a diamond wedding band (American Gem Society 1998).

Of course, none of these rings are necessary or mandatory, but patriarchal history and the work of advertisers and other members of the wedding-industrial complex have been so effective in conveying their message that most newlyweds follow the norm. "May I have the rings please?" is a phrase most believe carries the authority of the church or synagogue and is integral to the wedding ceremony, making noncompliance unthinkable.

Lynn Ramsey, president of the Jewelry Information Center in Manhattan, a nonprofit association representing the fine jewelry industry, offers this rationale for purchasing expensive wedding jewelry:

> When you think about what [a diamond] represents—a union between two people that could last a lifetime—then it isn't very much money. And you can pass the ring on to your children. But you have to think about it differently than a car or fur coat, because [each] diamond is unique. (Reinholz 1996)

The bride also wears jewelry, and the bride and groom frequently give gifts of jewelry to the wedding party. Sold as markers of "one of life's most important rites of passage," infamous and upscale establishments such as Tiffany & Co. and Fortunoff set the standard for suitable and even "affordable" gifts. Typical choices are sterling silver cufflinks or money clips for the ushers and pearl earrings or silver or crystal necklaces and pendants for the bridesmaids. The total average expenditure per wedding on jewelry in the United States is nearly $5,000.

The Diamond Industry and
De Beers's Diamond International

Hidden behind the romance with diamond rings and wedding jewelry is an industry with a history steeped in intrigue, treachery, and vast wealth. Everyone from global capitalists to governments to political operatives to advertising agencies to jewelry stores is included. The mining, manufacturing, and marketing of diamonds has involved colonial wars, apartheid, racist violence, massive labor abuses, struggles between superpowers, the stability of nations, and the hiring of mercenary armies. This section offers a historical sketch of the leading players and interests and will provide a case study of the largest and most powerful diamond cartel: De Beers Diamond Mining International, based in South Africa.

"Diamonds are forever" the De Beers's ad claims, or at least DeBeers' hopes so. And they're not talking about Ian Fleming's James Bond novel *Diamonds are Forever* (1956), which Fleming based on the real DeBeers's story (Rubin 1997). Founded by Cecil Rhodes during the British colonial era in southern Africa in 1888, the modern De Beers organization was created and overseen by Sir Ernest Oppenheimer. His son, South African Harry Oppenheimer, as chairman of De Beers, went to great lengths in the 1950s to secure control of African diamond reserves,

> by enlisting Sir Percy Sillitoe, one of Britain's top counterespionage agents during World War II. . . . Sillitoe orchestrated an intelligence network of local informants along the smuggling trail, hired an army of mercenaries, and launched an all-out diamond war. The mercenaries laid booby traps, mined the border crossings, and ambushed the smugglers—predominantly Mandingo tribesmen and Lebanese—until they were persuaded to sell their wares to the De Beers buyers. (Rubin 1997, 54)

Since that time, De Beers Consolidated Mines Limited has grown and diversified to become what some now refer to as the Oppenheimer empire (Atkinson 1998). De Beers sold $4.8 billion in rough gems in 1996 and reported holdings of $8.47 billion in 1997, including diamonds, gold, copper, coal, other minerals, industrial, and finance.

With interests in nineteen African diamond mines in South Africa, Botswana, Namibia, and Tanzania, its Central Selling Organisation unit (CSO)—the "diamond cartel"—controls 80 percent of the world's rough diamond production. In addition to its current holdings, De Beers's technical resources are directed toward the "discovery of world-class deposits and the investigation of known deposits in Africa, Canada, Brazil, Europe, Australia, and Asia." Currently, De Beers is establishing prospecting bases in Angola, negotiating with the troubled Democratic Republic of Congo to purchase the Miba mine, and has started negotiations with China, Gabon, and Guinea for prospecting rights.

Its prime competitors include Russian, Angolan, Australian, and Canadian diamond producers. In 1997, De Beers brokered a deal with Almazy Rossii Sakha (ARS) of Russia to buy $550 million worth of uncut diamonds annually. This didn't happen without significant struggle, however. With the bulk of Russian diamonds under the control of the republic of Yakutia, a struggle ensued involving ARS, Moscow, and Yakutia to release nearly $300 million in diamonds to De Beers.

De Beers's top two sales markets are the United States and Japan, with the United States accounting for one-third of all sales. De Beers is currently actively pursuing markets in the Asia Pacific region and in Turkey, the Middle East, Pakistan, and India (which now accounts for 10 percent of world diamond demand). De Beers's chairman reports that marketing programs targeted at China, believed to have enormous potential, are currently achieving positive results (Oppenheimer 1998).

While De Beers maintains offices and associates in many countries—in much of Africa and in Switzerland (the corporate headquarters of De Beers Centenary, which controls the company's non-South African assets), the United Kingdom, Belgium, China, Israel, India, Russia, Canada, Ireland, Japan, Sweden, and Hong Kong—De Beers's roots remain in South Africa, where its past is intricately bound up with the that country's history, including its colonial and white supremacist history with apartheid. In reality, De Beers owes much of its wealth and success to the black South Africans who worked and slaved under apartheid in South African mines.

In Sierra Leone, Africa, where civil wars and mercenary armies have been funded by the government to provide access to diamond mining by multinational corporations, the people don't think of diamonds as symbols of love, romance, and commitment. As one reporter put it: "The diamond in Kono has always wielded greater authority than the local paramount chief or the state president or the foreign investors. Some people said that the diamond is alive, that is has a fire you can feel. Others said it is the fire of the devil" (Rubin 1997, 52). Workers for one of the smaller mining companies earn between "one and five dollars per day, plus some rice. . . . After all that labor, though, no ancient city would be discovered and no buildings would be erected; instead, hundreds of thousands of couples around the world would consecrate their engagements with the little stone ferreted out of the mud" (53).

Wedding Consulting

The older, two-income newlywed market has given rise to a new and very lucrative occupation: wedding consulting. "Women with careers want elaborate weddings—and can afford them—but don't have the time to invest in planning them" (Sherwin 1995, 30). This means that activities formerly the domain of family are becoming commodified in a way that redefines social relations and the hetero-gendered division of labor as business transactions.

You may remember the character Franck, played by Martin Short, in *Father of the Bride*. He was a caricature of an affected, upscale wedding consultant. This movie, a Touchstone production owned by Disney, was so successful that Disney modeled their wedding consulting business after it. The Walt Disney Corporation is a central player in the wedding-industrial complex. On one level Disney's contribution to the wedding market has been substantial historically with the production of children's animated films, many of which end with weddings, happily ever afters, and romantic promises. Now Disney has taken things a step farther; they have ten wedding consultants on staff at their new Fairy Tale Wedding Pavilion in Disneyland and Disney World—already the honeymoon capital of the United States—which marries 2,100 couples a year. The starting price for a fifty-guest wedding is $17,500 (Johnson 1992). The "Ultimate Fairy Tale Wedding" costs $100,000 and allows couples to reserve the Magic Kingdom for the "big event." The bride rides down Main Street in a glass carriage drawn by six white horses and is greeted by uniformed trumpeters and her "prince," who rides to the wedding on a white stallion (Dager 1997).

"There was a Disney wedding during our stay, actually, to which we were invited—via telecast. The groom, who had proposed here the previous year, gave the bride a gilt-edged Disney Cinderella book and a shopping trip to Treasure Island."

—Rapping, 1995

Walt Disney Company Holdings (1998)

Disney World
Disneyland
Anaheim Mighty Ducks (NHL)

Disney Interactive
ABC Online

ABC Television Network
ABC Productions
Walt Disney Television
Touchstone Television
Buena Vista Television
11 television stations, including Chicago,
Los Angeles, Houston, San Francisco,
New York, Philadelphia

Walt Disney Pictures
Caravan Pictures
Miramax Pictures
Buena Vista Pictures Distribution
Touchstone Pictures
Hollywood Pictures

Walt Disney Records
Hollywood Records

The Disney Channel
ESPN and ESPN2
Lifetime
Arts and Entertainment

Buena Vista Home Video
Walt Disney Home Video

Disney Press
Hyperion Books
Hyperion Press

ABC radio networks (3,400 affiliates and
110 million listeners each week)

10 FM and 11 AM radio stations,
including New York, San Francisco, Los
Angeles, Detroit, Atlanta, Chicago, Dallas

7 daily newspapers, with a circulation of
744,000, including *Fort Worth Star-
Telegram* and *Kansas City Star*

Magazines:
Women's Wear Daily
Los Angeles Magazine
Disney Adventures
W Magazine
Discover
Family Fun
Family PC
Institutional Investor

Chilton Trade Publications
Fairchild Publications

Percentage holdings in:
Berkshire Hathaway Inc.
State Farm Insurance

Table 2.4
Disney holdings

The wedding industry reports that wedding consulting has become one of the hottest segments of the industry. Independent consultants can go into business with as little as $3,000 (Gite 1992; Sherwin 1995). With some research, promotional materials, and a link to either the Association of Bridal Consultants (ABC) or National Bridal Service (NBS), which offer courses and workshops, almost anyone can enter this field. ABC currently claims over one thousand members in forty-eight states and ten foreign countries and charges $200 for membership; NBS boasts eight hundred members, with a membership fee of $300. Most bridal consultants charge between $25 an hour to 15 percent of the total bridal package, making consulting a very profitable undertaking.

In a recent article in *Black Enterprise* entitled "Here Comes the Money," the author presents a picture of wedding consulting as extremely lucrative. Targeted to the African-American entrepreneur, the article lays out the possibilities for catering to the African-American wedding market. "Wedding planners charge 15 percent of the total wedding costs, raking in, on average, $20,000 to $50,000 a year" (Watts 1994, 1). Typically, in the wedding industry literature, articles targeting a black audience see the black marriage market as untapped and lucrative.

Perhaps the most elite of all wedding consultants, Martha Stewart has teamed up—tied the knot—with Macy's to offer wedding-planning seminars at Macy's stores across the nation. The top lure for brides is the chance to win a personal consultation with Stewart herself (Fitzgerald 1994). Stewart, however, shares her upscale status with another famous wedding consultant, Colin Cowie, whose primary clientele are movie stars. Referred to as "Hollywood's premiere wedding designer," Cowie charges a minimum of $12,000; his fees have often exceeded $250,000 and have on occasion reached a million. When Cowie was asked by *People* what advice he could give to the "average" bride, he responded: "Style is not related to money. . . . I've spent a million dollars in an afternoon, but I've been just as happy spending a fraction of that" (1995a, 136).

Destination Weddings and Honeymoons

One of the hottest new trends in weddings is that of the destination wedding—or the "weddingmoon," as Sandals Resorts calls them. Rather than invite two hundred fifty guests to a reception that costs an average of $8,000 combined with the average cost of a honeymoon, $3,657, newlyweds are opting for weddings in "exotic" faraway places with a small group of family and friends. Some couples opt for this to avoid the emotional entanglements weddings frequently provoke with family members when they struggle over guest lists. "Listen," confides one wedding planner, "there are people who will pay anything to just get away from the politics of that . . ." (Reynolds 1992, 2). The most popular locations are the Caribbean, Hawaii, and Disney World—which, coincidentally, also have the least complicated legal marriage requirements.

The entire wedding party, including guests, celebrates the occasion with the newlyweds and then either stays with them for an extended vacation or leaves following the wedding, allowing the couple to have a honeymoon. The market for destination weddings doubled between 1991 and 1995 (*Modern Bride* 1996). While the market dictated this trend to some degree, the travel industry also played a key role, marketing destination weddings as a way to capitalize on the "recession-proof" wedding industry. With the growth of this trend, travel agents now refer to themselves as "wedding travel specialists" (Dogar 1997).

Another form of destination wedding is the currently popular post-*Titanic* cruise business, with businesses such as Carnival Cruise Lines staging more than sixteen hundred weddings last year (Reynolds 1992). Even Disney has recently entered the cruise business. And, of course, a Disney wedding is another example of a destination wedding.

Bride's magazine reports that 99 percent of its readers take a honeymoon trip. The average amount spent on foreign trips is $4,048 and on domestic trips, $3,266. Newlyweds generally stay about eight days and also pay for most of the expense themselves. *Bride's* readers tend to be white and more affluent than the average newlywed (*Bride's* 1997).

Generally, islands are "in" for honeymoons. Popular sites in order of popularity are the Caribbean, Hawaii, Florida, and Mexico, followed by domestic trips (*Bride's* 1997). Maui, Hawaii, for example, reports that it now maintain a $50 million-a-year wedding industry (*Travel Weekly* 1996), which creates hundreds of small and big business jobs on the island.

Brochure handed out at New York Bridal Expo, March 1997:

"You can run but you can't hide from . . . the time of your life! Survival New York & Paintball Long Island . . . Bachelor Parties. . . . Come experience the thrill of helicopter assaults and the tank charges. . . ."

"We think wedding consultants should be right up there with doctors and lawyers. After all, they're organizing what is probably the most emotional day of your life" (Doger 1997).

—Houston wedding consultant

Hotels in the islands are also thriving as a growing proportion of visitors have their weddings and honeymoons at this destination. They even provide flowers, video, and catering, maximizing their profits. Supplementing this successful business is the independent coordinator or wedding consultant. Since these weddings take place far from the couple's home, the services of a consultant are even more important. Couples come to Maui not only from the United States but also in large numbers from Japan, Europe, New Zealand, and Australia. Even the Hyatt Regency on Maui has just put in a wedding chapel (Salkever 1995; *Travel Weekly* 1996).

Sandals Group Resorts

One award-winning resort that has been enormously successful in attracting newlyweds to the Caribbean is Sandals. Marketing themselves as "luxury resorts for [heterosexual] couples only," Sandals has hotels in Jamaica, Antigua, St. Lucia, and the Bahamas. The chairman of Sandals Group, Gordon (Butch) Stewart, recently received an award for "Number One Independent Resort Group in the World" at the World Travel Awards organized by *Tour and Travel News and Travel Trade Gazette.* In accepting the award, Stewart attributed the success of Sandals to the teamwork and dedication of their four thousand employees and said that "during the recent recession, Sandals refurbished and improved its hotels" (Gregory 1994). The result has been a doubling of their matrimonial business. According to a Sandals wedding coordinator, Sandals's staff handles an average of twenty-four weddings per day among their six hotels (Gregory 1994).

Sandals advertising stands out in most publications, characterized by fluorescent orange and pink colors with splashes of yellow, purple, and brilliant green. The ads are very effective attention-getters and show collages of couples throughout. Most bridal magazines carry them, as do other magazines. Enter a travel agency or attend a bridal show and you'll find their advertising booklets prominently displayed. What also stands out in their publications is the prevalence of white couples. In one 112-page booklet describing their "ultra-all-inclusive [meaning all services included] luxury resorts for couples only," they show photographs of approximately 708 heterosexual couples; 694 are white. Put another way, at these resort hotels for couples-only, all but fourteen of the couples were people of color paired with other people of color, usually of the same ethnicity. There were no interracial couples pictured.

All the servants, however—whether they be bartenders, waiters/waitresses, masseuses, drivers, hotel clerks, facial experts, or boat operators—were people of color. The extremely obvious message here is that Sandals Resorts are for white couples who can luxuriate in the Caribbean Ocean while being served by local people of color. One can only wonder what the earnings are of the workers at these resorts for which Mr. Stewart received such acclaim and what the difference is between his earnings and those of the workers who made it possible for Sandals to gain such acclaim.

In *A Small Place*, a scathing critique of the tourism industry in the Caribbean, noted author Jamaica Kincaid writes:

> . . . you stay in this place (Antigua) where the sun always shines and where the climate is deliciously hot and dry for the four to ten days you are going to be staying there; and since you are on your holiday, since you are a tourist, the thought of what it might be like for someone who had to live day in, day out in a place that suffers constantly from drought, and so has to watch carefully every drop of fresh water used (while at the same time surrounded by a sea and an ocean) . . . must never cross your mind. (1989, 4)

What also may never cross your mind is that these resorts are built on islands that once were centers for the slave trade, which other countries referred to as their colonies. Today, nonindigenous corporations extract enormous wealth and resources from countries where the vast majority live in poverty. These are some of the underlying historical and material conditions upon which the travel industry depends.

The Secondary Wedding Market

Recognizing the magnitude and promise of the transnational wedding industry, businesses interested in developing a future clientele also target newlyweds indirectly. As you will see in the following section, the secondary wedding market is, for the most part, sizable and undocumented and covers everything from "My Size Bride Barbie" to True Value Hardware, Ford Motor Company, and Bell Atlantic yellow pages. Advertising using wedding images to target newlyweds is virtually everywhere.

The secondary wedding market is made up of companies using white weddings to sell products that are only *indirectly* related to them. For example, while Metropolitan Life uses white weddings in its ads, life insurance is not a direct wedding item but is something that a married couple might purchase years later, after acquiring some property or having children. Numerous companies use this strategy to secure future consumption. For example, Parke-Davis now sponsors booths at bridal expos marketing family planning and birth control to newlyweds. Even Viagra marketers are targeting newlyweds of all ages.

Case Study: Mattel and the Toy Industry

The marketing of wedding products does not begin with adult women. Toy manufacturers, for one, have seized on the current wedding market and the opportunity to develop future consumers by producing a whole variety of wedding toys featuring the "classic" white wedding and sold during Saturday-morning children's television shows.

Toy companies, generally part of large conglomerates that also own related commodities such as travel or cosmetics, work to secure future markets for all their products through the selling of wedding toys. For example, Toy Biz, which is owned by the same company as Revlon, produces a product called the "Caboodles Wedding Playset" featuring not only a wedding but also "free" makeup for the future bride. Of course, it should be clear by now that the primary target of wedding products is girls and young women.

Mattel, the world's largest toymaker and a major multinational corporation, has offices and facilities in thirty-six countries and sells products in one hundred fifty nations. Their major toy brand, accounting for 40 percent of their sales, is the Barbie doll—all one hundred twenty different versions of her. They also own Fisher-Price, Disney entertainment lines, Hot Wheels and Matchbox cars, Tyco Toys, Cabbage Patch Kids, and games (Hoover's 1998; PR Newswire 1998). Mattel's primary manufacturing facilities are located in China, Indonesia, Italy, Malaysia, and Mexico, employing mostly women of color and at substandard wages. Annually, Mattel makes about 100 million Barbie dolls and earns revenues of $1.9 billion for their El Segundo, California, company. Their CEO, Jill Barad, age 46, earns $1,545,511 annually; they spend approximately $140 million per year on advertising (Hoover's 1998). Compare this to the young Chinese female workers they employ, who live in dormitories, sometimes work with dangerous chemicals, work long hours, and earn $1.81 a day (Holstein et al. 1996).

Bridal Barbies and bridal gowns and accessories are popular items for toy consumers. "Never married but always prepared, Barbie has about 30 bridal gowns in her closet, with new ones released each year" (Tousignant 1996, 8C). Their "My Size Bride Barbie" is a recent addition. This three-foot-tall doll comes dressed in a wedding gown that also fits young girls sizes 4–10. It retails for $149 and features a white, blond, blue-eyed, thin, and "pretty" Barbie doll and packaging that includes a photo of a little girl who looks very much like Barbie.

In 1996, *Dateline NBC, The Nation,* and *U.S. News & World Report* provided exposés on Asian sweatshops, where Barbies are produced by poor children for a market they will never be able to enter. "Mattel makes tens of millions of Barbies a year in China, where young female Chinese workers who have migrated thousands of miles from home are alleged to earn less than the minimum wage of $1.99 a day" (Holstein et al. 1996, 50). In Indonesia, where it is illegal to unionize, workers earn $2.25 per day. "It would take such a worker about a month to earn enough to buy Mattel's cK Calvin Klein Barbie, and twenty-eight years to make the C.E.O.'s daily salary" (Press 1996, 10).

Efforts by Mattel's Mexican employees to unionize have been met with extremely repressive actions:

"Fashion designer Vera Wang has taken her first steps down the catwalk of dolldom with a series of designer Barbies. Know in today's world of haute couture as the premier designer of bridal gowns, Wang has extended her creative talents to include the world's top fashion doll, dressing the honey-blond fashion maven in one of her signature gowns."

—Denise I. O'Neil, *Chicago Sun-Times,* June 12, 1998.

> Upon entering the plant, Rodriguez says, her purse was searched and she was taken into a room by a security guard. She and two other workers say they were coercively interrogated, accused of passing out subversive materials, detained against their will until the next morning and prevented from going to the bathroom or making phone calls to their families. In the end . . . [they were told] they would have to quit their jobs or go to prison. (Press 1996, 10)

While it is not illegal to organize in Mexico, the actions of company officials have a quieting effect on workers interested in protecting their rights.

In a recent article in the *Wall Street Journal*, "Toy Business Focuses More on Marketing and Less on New Ideas" (Pereira 1996), the author makes reference to Mattel's revenues and profit margins:

> Mattel reaped $1.4 billion in sales last year from Barbie and her spinoffs, by far the biggest line in all of toy land. Gross profit margins on licensed figurines can run 50%, what with the modest cost of making them; most are produced abroad and don't require much investment in plant and equipment. (A1)

This article was only critical of Mattel's conservative approach to innovation. The bulk of Mattel's expenses, it is reported here, can be attributed to marketing and product development and design, not to labor and production costs.

In 1988, Mattel "married" Disney. At that time, Mattel contracted to become Disney's lead toy licensee. In 1996, Mattel and Disney created another alliance, a three-year licensing pact for Disney's television and film properties. This arrangement gives Mattel exclusive rights for the production of toys tied to Disney films. With Disney products viewed as highly profitable, competition by toy companies vying for such contracts is stiff. Considering Disney's history in the production of "happily-ever-after" films where the heroine generally finds and marries her Prince Charming, the secondary wedding market has become even stronger with this corporate "wedding."

"Ms. Barad [CEO] . . . has also replaced Mattel's steady work hours with a schedule that is more flexible than Ballet Recital Barbie. Every Friday is now a half-day at Mattel, and employees can take off four Fridays of their choosing each year. They get 16 hours off every year to volunteer at a local school. In addition to vacations, for most employees in Mattel's American offices there is a company-wide break at the end of December that lasts two weeks."

—Adam Bryant, "A Toyshop That Doesn't Forget to Play," New York Times, October 11, 1998, p. 3.4

Disney and the Secondary Wedding Market

One of the most dramatic examples in the wedding-industrial complex is the Walt Disney Co. Not only are they involved in the *primary* wedding market, but they are also central players in the *secondary* wedding market, serving a powerful role in securing future consumers by catering directly to both children and adults through film, television, theme parks, sports franchises, and publishing companies. Disney is the world's second-largest media conglomerate, after Time Warner, with annual revenues exceeding $22 billion, 50,000 employees, 10 collective bargaining agreements, 32 unions, and holdings that are extremely diverse. For example, they own Walt Disney Pictures, Touchstone Pictures, Caravan Pictures, Miramax Films, Buena Vista Pictures Distribution, and Hollywood Pictures. They control ABC Television Network, a variety of television stations in major media markets, Walt Disney Television, Touchstone Television, and Buena Vista Television. Disney maintains ABC radio networks, which reach 100 million listeners each week, major market radio stations, the Disney Channel, ESPN and ESPN2, Lifetime, and the Arts and Entertainment Network. If this weren't enough, they also own Disneyland, Disney World, the Epcot Center, Disney stores, ABC Online, Disney Interactive, and a wide variety of magazines and newspapers, including *Women's Wear Daily* (see Table 2.4).

Founded in 1923 by Walter and Roy Disney, Walt Disney Productions established its fame with an animated film mouse called Mickey Mouse. With the enormous success of their animated short films, the Disney brothers went on to create Disneyland in 1955. Although the Disney Company stayed under family control for many years, in 1984 in the wake of a hostile corporate takeover many modifications were made to the corporate structure. New goals were established for the company's future. It shifted its consumer focus, expanded and diversified into related fields, changed from Walt Disney Productions to Walt Disney Company, and hired the current CEO, Michael Eisner. Eisner has become one of the most powerful figures nationally with control of this media empire, stock options worth almost $200 million, and an annual salary of $750,000.

Disney's long history with the secondary wedding market is wrapped up in its

Mattel Inc. shareholders on Wednesday voted down a proposal to link top executives' pay to child labor practices at the toymaker's overseas manufacturing operations. . . . "Our position was that not only do we have certainly the most aggressive monitor plan in the toy industry, but we are the first international consumer products company to introduce independent third-party monitoring on a worldwide basis . . . the initiative was essentially redundant."

Associated Press 1998, B1

"I saw hundreds of women and children stuffing, cutting, dressing, and assembling Barbie dolls—as well as Lion Kings my daughter worships and other Disney properties that dazzle me. Many of these factory workers suffer from pains in their hands, necks, and shoulders. Others experience nausea and dizziness and suffer from hair and memory loss. They sleep badly. The most common complaints . . . are of shortage of breath and infections in and around the throat. . . . 'I am an old woman even before my twentieth birthday.'"

—Foek 1997, p. 9

dominance of children's films, particularly animated films, for many decades. Famous examples include *Beauty and the Beast, The Little Mermaid, Snow White and the Seven Dwarfs,* and *Cinderella.* The vast majority of Disney children's films have "happily-ever-after" endings in which the (usually white) damsel-in-distress finds her handsome prince and, by the end of the film, weds. For many years, Disney films have been equated with the beautiful maiden finding her Prince Charming, marrying, and living happily ever after. As mentioned earlier, this is the foundation for Disney's success in the primary wedding market with their Fairy Tale Wedding business.Beyond their children's films, Disney has also produced *Father of the Bride* and *Muriel's Wedding.*

Not without controversy, Disney's role in the wedding industry is, at best, contradictory. On the one hand Disney has for decades cultivated a wedding market through their dominance in popular film. They've taken this market and turned it into a lucrative wedding and honeymoon business in Disney World and Disneyland. Their adult wedding films tend to be blockbusters, further securing their hold on the wedding industry, and their television shows on ABC are among those beginning or ending their seasons with a wedding. The Lifetime Channel, another one of their media holdings, regularly features both celebrity wedding and other wedding shows.

On the other hand, this same media conglomerate has been the target of numerous protests and boycotts on the part of the religious right. Because of their liberal domestic partners' policy, gay and lesbian employees are able to get a variety of benefits from the Disney Company. They also allowed the production of the first sitcom with an openly lesbian main character on a major network with the showing of *Ellen* on ABC.

But they've also been in trouble with the labor movement. In 1996, Charles Kernaghan and the National Labor Committee exposed Disney's use of sweatshops in Haiti and other parts of the world in the production of Disney products. With their alliance with Mattel, the reach of this production into other offshore locations where labor practices are less than desirable has put Disney's image of family fun and loveable cartoon characters into jeopardy.

The Perfect Marriage...
Tartar Control *Plus* Whitening!

An example of how
white weddings are
used in advertising.

The Tertiary Wedding Market

The tertiary wedding market is made up of those companies that have little or no relationship to the wedding market or to newlyweds but make use of wedding imagery to capture the imaginations of potential consumers. The romance, promise, and morality of white weddings secure product consumption, especially by women who associate this image with something positive and trustworthy. White weddings appear in a vast array of advertising for products such as Aetna Retirement Services, Buick, One-A-Day Vitamins, Pepto Bismol, Estée Lauder perfume, Colgate-Palmolive products, Bell Atlantic, Buick, Keds, General Electric, McDonald's, Tylenol, Bayer Aspirin, Pepsi, Ford, Chevrolet, Toyota, 10-10-321 long-distance service, and Midas Muffler, to name a few.

There are currently no data available to measure the size and scope of the tertiary wedding market. Suffice it to say, it's probably worth millions.

The State

The state plays a major role in affecting how we think about and engage in the practice of wedding. In regulating marriage materially via civil law, the state injects its presence into the wedding ceremony through licensing practices and fees, establishing who is legally "qualified" to officiate a wedding, and charges for blood tests and name changes. The state also protects its interests through miscegenation, domestic relations, and other laws regarding what constitutes legitimate marriage. For example, New York State domestic relations laws assert that a "legal" marriage can only occur between one man and one woman.[5] But it wasn't until 1972 that it was found necessary to include this clarification, leading us to question, after hundreds of years without this clause, what made this exclusion a necessity in 1972. Several explanations are plausible here. The lesbian and gay rights movement and the feminist movement were very active at this time, pressuring all sorts of laws for inclusive language. Foremost in these efforts was the push for an Equal Rights Amendment (ERA) to insert "women" into the language of the Constitution. The gendered division of labor was also being challenged at this historical moment vis-à-vis feminism, and the state asserted its interests by preserving marriage as a solely heterogendered institution.

With state domestic relations laws stating such things as "[the state considers] marriage the cornerstone of organized society" and "the state regards with a jealous eye any effort to interfere in this relation," it's no wonder similar ideas are often inscribed in the wedding ceremony and in the officiating comments of the clergy. As the point of entry to marriage, the wedding signals compliance with these regulating practices, consent to the heterogendered division of labor the traditional wedding enacts, and access to the many benefits and rewards of this institution. "Over a ten-year period, an [unmarried and partnered] worker earning $40,000 a year may earn as much as $55,800 less in benefits than a married co-worker" (Demian 1997). Few newlyweds have read these laws or are aware that marriage, according to these statutes, is a relation among man, woman, and the state.[6] It is well within the realm of state and federal legislators' influence, then, to engage in public debate about the morality (or politics) of marriage or the need for welfare mothers to marry. The effect of this engagement can best be seen in attempts by newlyweds to create rituals that signify their distance from lower-class practices. Regardless of their incomes, couples frequently purchase wedding services far in excess of their ability to pay. The law is a powerful vehicle to control challenges to patriarchal authority.

The state plays another significant role and one even less obvious than any previously mentioned. Through free trade agreements such as NAFTA[7] and GATT,[8] the state creates the conditions by which exploitative offshore labor practices are undertaken in the manufacturing of such products as wedding gowns, gifts, and wedding toys. And the state features in the travel industry to the extent that it regulates tourism particularly in conjunction with transnational corporations and national security interests.

In 1997 the U.S. Congress voted overwhelmingly to pass the Defense of Marriage Act (DOMA) (see Appendix for full text), changing the role of the federal government in defining "marriage" as a "legal union between one man and one woman as husband and wife"—usually a right reserved for states—and prohibiting the legalization of same-sex marriage for federal purposes and allowing states to ignore a same-sex marriage from another state. "Although the marriage contract is governed by state law, the federal government uses marital status as the qualification for more than 1,049 federally registered rights and responsibilities" (Partners 1997). With the passage of this law, the U.S. government essentially asserted that state and federal rights and responsibilities connected to legal marriage be denied anyone who is *not married*—singles, lesbians, gay men, cohabitating heterosexuals, siblings living together, etc. In preparation for passage of this bill, the U.S. Government Accounting Office (GAO) identified all federal laws in which marital status is a factor. They found thirteen categories: Social Security (which includes related programs, housing, and food stamps); veterans' benefits; taxation; civilian and military benefits; employment benefits; immigration and naturalization laws; Indians; trade, commerce, and intellectual property; financial disclosure and conflict of interest; crimes and family violence; loans, guarantees, and payments in agriculture; federal natural resources and related laws; and miscellaneous laws (Bedrick 1997) (see Appendix for listings). In most cases, these laws assume the presence of a marital relationship. To provide a sense for the extent to which these laws reward "legal" marriage, I've provided a few examples. Under the first category, Social Security law, benefits to domestic partners only continue if those partners are legally married. Laws pertaining to Old Age, Survivors, and Disability Insurance (OASDI) are written in terms of the rights of husbands and wives, widows and widowers. Married persons are considered "essential" to individuals receiving Medicaid benefits and are therefore eligible for medical assistance themselves. In the National Affordable Housing program intended to assist "first-time home buyers," this category is defined as "an individual and his or her spouse"(Defense of Marriage Act 1997).

The second grouping, veterans' benefits, awards husbands and wives many opportunities based on their marital status. For instance, a surviving spouse is entitled to monthly dependency and indemnity compensation payments when the veteran's death is service-connected. When the death is not service-connected, the spouse is entitled to receive a monthly pension. The spouse of a veteran is also entitled to compensation if a veteran disappears. Furthermore, spouses of certain veterans are entitled to medical care, National Service Life Insurance, preference in federal employment, and interment in national cemeteries. And, finally, spouses of veterans who die from a service-connected disability are entitled to educational assistance, job counseling, training, and placement services.

Laws pertaining to Indians[9] (Native Americans) insert property rights into the

> *"The Romans had legal protections for their military soldiers who were in holy unions (same-sex marriages). In fact, Roman law had required the Jewish council, the Sanhedrin, to come up with its own law to punish Jews who stoned or defamed lesbian/gay couples of Roman citizenship."*
>
> —Rev. Timm Peterson, Ph.D. (Demian 1998)

lives of native peoples on the basis of marital status. "Various laws set out the rights to tribal property of white men marrying Indian women, or of Indian women marrying white men" (Defense of Marriage Act 1997, 6). This group of laws also gives relocation benefits to spouses who relinquish life estates.

Particularly poignant benefits the government awards on the basis of marital status are visitation rights in hospitals and prisons, bereavement leaves, burial determination, child custody, domestic violence protection, sick leave to care for a partner, and medical decisions on behalf of a partner. These rights and privileges are only granted to "legally" married couples. Anyone living outside of this arrangement must either make costly legal arrangements or depend on the mercy and sensitivity of the governing institutions for access to these protections.

The centrality of marital status to "organized society" cannot be understated given the significance of these laws to the everyday lives of U.S. citizens and immigrants. The state has a substantial stake in heterosexual marriage and protects and preserves its interests in a multitude of laws, policies, and practices. Even the U.S. Postal Service recognizes the revenue potential of the wedding market and regularly staffs booths at regional bridal shows. The postage costs for wedding and shower invitations as well as for thank-you notes are substantial.

Religion

Religions vary in the meaning they attach to the wedding, but all reserve the right to require certain practices and beliefs regarding the wedding ceremony as well as the institution of marriage. Many religions view a marriage as a religious institution and not the domain of the state. Yet religious ceremonies do not carry the weight of law. Newlyweds must also obtain a state license in order to have access to the material rewards of this arrangement. While religions interact with the state in legalizing a marriage, their power rests in legitimizing marriage through moral teachings.

Compliance with religious doctrine can be seen clearly in the selection of readings used during the ceremony itself as well as in the comments offered by the presiding clergy. The wedding becomes a site for the ritual enactment of religious doc-

"The freedom to marry has long been recognized as one of the vital personal rights essential to the orderly pursuit of happiness by free men."

—Chief Justice Earl Warren writing for the majority, *Loving v. Virginia*, 1967.

"I have been privileged on many occasions to work with a substantial number of ministers whose Washington churches today are referred to as 'African American.' . . . I ran into one of these fine ministers. . . . He was saying, 'Are you going home tomorrow?' I told him I thought I was. . . . I asked him . . . if he had a message for the folks back home. And he said, 'I sure do. Tell them that God created Adam and Eve—not Adam and Steve.'"

—Senator Jesse Helms, September 9, 1996, with regard to the Defense of Marriage Act.

trine, shoring up the stake the church has in heterosexual marriage and in a patriarchal social order that ensures a heterogendered division of labor and women's continued function as the property of men. This is embodied especially in the "giving away" of the bride from father (son, brother, or even both parents) to husband and in the "taking" of the husband's last name. In many ceremonies, the naming exceeds just the taking of the last name. Frequently, the newlyweds are announced as "For the first time ever, Mr. and Mrs. Ralph Reed."

In June 1998, southern Baptists voted to uphold patriarchal marriage as the centerpiece of the Baptist faith by declaring that a woman should "submit herself graciously" to her husband. Ironically, southern Baptists, who would find the greatest popular culture support for their position in Disney films, toys, and theme parks—especially Disney's Fairy Tale Wedding Pavilion at Disney World— have launched a boycott against the Disney Company for what they consider to be a significant decline in moral values. Disney has in recent years supported a benefits package for domestic partnerships and has, through its holdings—ABC, Disney World, Touchstone, and Miramax—provided both film and television offerings that southern Baptists consider unacceptable.[10] Most notable of these was the television sitcom *Ellen*, which featured a lesbian lead character and lesbian and gay themes. The Church of the Nazarene and Presbyterian Church in America have also voiced their concerns over Disney's moral direction and have joined the boycott. "It has become clear that the Disney Corporation is on a deliberate course of promoting the homosexual agenda and marginalizing the evangelical and conservative church and making them seem irrelevant to our culture" (Toalston 1998).

Religions frequently set the rules for personal and social behavior and relationships. In particular, they organize and regulate marriage, monogamy, patriarchy, and police any violations of religious law.

Mass Media

The role of the mass media is primarily ideological and comprised of what sociologist Howard Becker calls "consciousness industries." In other words, their task is to provide the public with information and materials that help shape how we

view the world, ourselves, and the values we live by. They provide the symbols, myths, images, and ideas by which we constitute dominant culture.

When the work they do involves weddings and marriage, what is significant is the degree to which they make use of these images, the interests they serve, and the effect they have on our imaginations and values. Given the shrinking of media ownership down to six major conglomerates and the diversity of their holdings, these messages tend not to vary much. Disney is a perfect example of this, with its control of multimedia, home video, book publishing, motion pictures, magazines, TV and cable, retail, sports teams, newspapers, music, insurance, petroleum and natural gas, and theme parks and resorts. Mass media are used by the privileged to define or legitimize entitlements by producing certain belief systems, based largely on myths and stereotypes. These entitlements refer to the rights of certain groups within society to have greater or lesser access to resources and institutions.

The staging of weddings in television shows, weekly reporting on weddings in the press, magazine reports on celebrity weddings, advertising, and popular adult and children's movies with wedding themes or weddings inserted all work together to teach us how to think about weddings, marriage, heterosexuality, race, gender, and labor. Through the application of the heterosexual imaginary, the media cloak most representations of weddings in signifiers of romance, purity, morality, promise, affluence or accumulation, and whiteness. Many newlyweds today experience their weddings as stars of a fairy-tale movie in which they are scripted, videotaped, and photographed by paparazzi wedding-goers. Even Kodak and Fuji offer disposable "wedding" cameras for placement on reception tables, ensuring that no moment in this spectacle will be overlooked.

In Chapter 3, I discuss the key role of bridal magazines in the primary wedding market and the wedding-ideological complex. As you will see, these periodicals depend upon signifiers of elegance, opulence, and traditional femininity and, with the exception of *Signature Bride,* also emphasize whiteness. Bridal magazines are a central site for demonstrating how the wedding industry is bound up with the accumulation of wealth and the perpetuation of a class, gender, and racial hierarchies.

"Still pregnant brides shouldn't expect widespread acceptance, especially from the clergy. [A couple from Syracuse] were married in a Catholic ceremony, but not in her family church; the priest there was known for ordering pregnant brides not to wear white. . . . Given all the discomfort, one might wonder why brides don't just put the whole thing off. For one reason, wedding plans have their own momentum. Postponement 'was my greatest fear,' explains the bride's mother. 'We'd put down deposits, we'd sent out the invitations.' . . . 'Given the alternative,' says Miss Manners, 'a wedding is very appropriate for the pregnant bride.'"

—Mieher 1993, p. A1

Conclusion

The contemporary white wedding under transnational capitalism is, in effect, a mass-marketed, homogeneous, assembly-line production with little resemblance to the utopian vision many participants hold. With enormous profit-making ventures dependent upon this market and newlyweds caught up in the machinery of the wedding production, the focus is on the alienating spectacle of accumulation being created. "The whole life of those societies in which modern conditions of production prevail presents itself as an immense accumulation of *spectacles*. All that once was directly lived has become mere representation" (Debord 1995, 12). The engine driving the wedding market has mostly to do with the the romancing of heterosexuality in the interests of capitalism. The social relations at stake—love, community, commitment, and family—become alienated from the production of the wedding spectacle, while practices reinforcing a heterogendered and racial division of labor, white supremacy, the private sphere as women's work, and women as property are reinforced.

The design of these rituals secures a heterogendered division of labor with the bride, socialized since childhood, as the domestic planner, showpiece of the groom's potential wealth and producer of future workers, while the groom represents final decisionmaker—patriarchal authority—and passive recipient of the bride's service. He's in charge of the (honeymoon) travel plans. The system also sets up the bride as primary consumer and the marriage promise as integral to the accumulation of private property, particularly for whites, who have significant economic advantage in American society. Ruth Frankenberg, in her ground-breaking book *White Women, Race Matters: The Social Construction of Whiteness* (1993), defines whiteness as

> a set of locations that are historically, socially, politically, and culturally produced and, moreover, are intrinsically linked to unfolding relations of domination. Naming "whiteness" displaces it from the unmarked, unnamed status that is itself an effect of its dominance. Among the effects on white people both of race privilege and of the dominance of

"Across the street from the church, more than a dozen anti-gay protesters waved signs with messages such as 'God Hates Fags.'... 'I came to spread some truth in this orgy of lies,' said [one protester] from a Baptist church in Topeka, Kan., whose members regularly engage in anti-homosexual picketing at funerals. One protester yelled: 'Mathew was wicked!'"

Associated Press Report on the funeral for Mathew Shepard, the young man who was murdered in Wyoming for being gay.

whiteness are their seeming normativity, their structured invisibility....
To look at the social construction of whiteness ... is to look head-on at a
site of dominance. (6)

The heterosexual imaginary circulating throughout the wedding-industrial complex masks the ways it secures racial, class, and sexual hierarchies. For instance, in nearly all of the examples offered here, the wedding industry depends upon the availability of cheap labor from developing nations with majority populations made up of people of color. The wealth garnered by white transnational corporations both relies on racial hierarchies, exploiting people and resources of communities of color (Africa, China, Haiti, Mexico, South Asia), and perpetuates them in the marketing of the wedding industry.

With nearly half of all marriages ending in divorce and the historical necessity of marriage diminishing, the wedding market "needs" the fantasy of the once-in-a-lifetime extravaganza/spectacle or it would cease to exist. How this fantasy is created is the work of the wedding-ideological complex and the focus of the next two chapters.

Companies refusing to grant permission to reprint their ads here:

Esteé Lauder
Phillip Morris/Virginia Slims
Vera Wang
Mattel (Barbie)
Disney
De Beers
Kenneth Cole

After indicating they would send a copy of their magazine, and following several faxed requests, *Vows: The Wedding Industry Trade Journal* did not send a copy of their publication.

"Never mind that people who've been divorced by 30 blithely refer to those aborted unions as their 'starter marriages,' that the rate of divorce tripled between 1970 and 1995, that a third of all babies today are born 'out of wedlock'... People still love a good party."

—Bart Nagel and Karen Huff, "Something Old, Something New," *Might*, March/April 1997, 48.

Chapter Three

Romancing the Clone

The **White** Wedding

"Match a pretty girl with a handsome guy. It's true love, now don't be shy. Dress them in a tux and a wedding gown. . . . They're the happiest couple in town! Next a chapel wedding for the bride and groom, then send them off on their honeymoon. Now move them into their family home . . . add special stickers to make it their own! The time has come for a sweet surprise . . . a dear little baby with love in her eyes! Inside! A baby for you after saying 'I do!'."

"Family Corners" toy by Mattel, 1994

"People who are ugly are not worthy of a wedding!"

the wedding singer in The Wedding Singer

The first quote opening this chapter comes from the back of a box for a doll named Ryan of the "Family Corners" series made by Mattel. Ryan is one of four potential groom dolls children can select to go with any one of four bride dolls. In addition to the family-values position in this passage, the four male dolls and the four female dolls each represent different ethnic groups. While the option is available for children to pair bride and groom whichever way they choose, Mattel doesn't want to leave anything to chance. The photos on the back of the box show each of the four male dolls by name and clothing, the four female dolls by name and clothing, and then provide "appropriate" pairings of each of the grooms with the corresponding bride of the same race or ethnicity. Since all the dolls represented are relatively light-skinned, their pairing by the more easily discernible hair-color differences—blonds with blonds, brunettes with brunettes, redheads with redheads—masks the racial pairings in evidence in these photos. In this example, children are discouraged from imagining interracial or interethnic marriage and same-sex pairings. Instead, the mythology of sameness concerning what counts as a family is

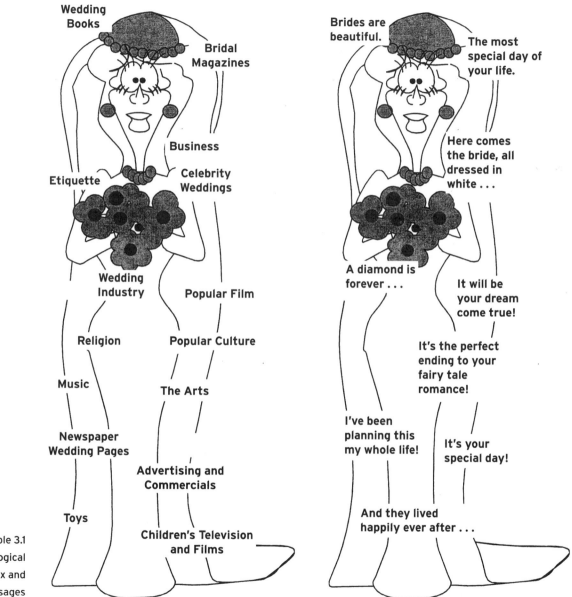

Table 3.1
Wedding Ideological
Complex and
Messages

instilled, making all other manifestations or configurations unimaginable. Nicola Field, in her recent book *Over the Rainbow*, explains the motivation and consequences of perpetuating this notion of family:

> The idea of the family as a protective haven is a myth, the family unit cannot provide the haven it promises. On the contrary, we can never isolate ourselves from social and political relationships in the world. The places we choose to hide are always inseparably connected to the real world, the world they actually might encounter in school, and for some, in neighborhoods. It is not the failure, or the breakdown, of the family which causes our alienation, but the ever-disappointed hopes instilled in us as children. These hopes are false dreams of being cocooned and of belonging. (Field 1995, 27)

The cocooning Field refers to in this passage is a form of romance, living within the imaginary. This illusion of insularity and well-being is recreated through romantic mythology, keeping children from seeing and living in the real world. Romancing heterosexuality in a manner such as that of the "Family Corners" toy ensures an ongoing wedding market, preserves patriarchal authority, and secures racial separation and a heterogendered division of labor. It secures housework and family as the exclusive domain of women and keeps in place a dependence on men for the survival of the family. These constructions of social relations conceal from children an awareness of real-life variations and the opportunity to develop one of life's most valuable survival skills—the ability to imagine alternatives.

The second quote, from the movie *The Wedding Singer*, sets up one of the key organizing principles of the wedding market. All brides are beautiful! Estée Lauder has long used an advertising campaign for its perfume depicting a white, blond flower girl in a white dress looking up into the eyes of a white, blond bride in a white wedding gown. The only text in the ad says "Beautiful," establishing the white bride and the future bride as standard-bearers of what counts as beauty.

What's not said but is implied in bridal magazines, children's toys, popular film, television, and advertising is that something is wrong with people who do not marry. *The Wedding Singer*, the "Family Corners" toy, and the Estée Lauder ad all reinforce the same message: that brides are beautiful, grooms are handsome, and anyone who doesn't marry is ugly. With a few notable exceptions covered later in this chapter, what counts as beautiful is white, fair, thin, and female.

In the examples above, the effect for anyone who doesn't meet these standards can be moderate to severe, manifesting in everything from eating disorders to the toleration of domestic violence to labor abuses. Additionally, examples such as these perpetuate gender, racial, class, and sexuality hierarchies, setting up some groups to fare poorly in relation to dominant constructions of heterosexuality. The beliefs emanating from these sites legitimize oppressive treatment of those who are not in the center of these constructions through the objectification and trivialization of those who don't fit the script. In other words, the institution of heterosexuality as it is currently organized functions as a form of social control and depends upon the heterosexual imaginary to conceal its regulatory function and effects.

Women are taught from early childhood to plan for "the happiest day of their lives." Men are taught, by the absence of these socializing mechanisms, that their work is "other" than that. A brief stroll through toy catalogs conveys this message quite clearly. The pages for girls are easy to locate. They are the ones little boys distance themselves from, and they are coded with Barbie pink. This same color permeates most products targeted to female children, including bicycles and other toys that have no particular gender distinctions. The possibilities children learn to imagine are only as broad as their culture allows. Children are socialized to understand the importance of coupling—appropriate coupling—and what counts as beauty, what counts as women's work and men's work, and how to become good consumers by participating in those institutions that stimulate their interests and emotions and reap the most rewards. Many people believe that the advances of the women's movement have been absorbed and are no longer necessary. Examining these markets shows that there is still an enormous amount of ideological weight placed on gender differentiation.

Gender does not exist in a social vacuum. It is the central organizing concept for the institution of heterosexuality, setting the standards for male/female rela-

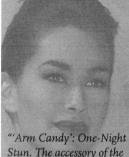

"'Arm Candy': One-Night Stun. The accessory of the 90's walks and talks (preferable only in monosyllables). The most important criteria are good looks and an absolute lack of expectations.

Arm candy. The phrase is bracing in its candor, implying a beautiful object to attach to your arm, for others to feast their eyes upon. In the image-obsessed 1990's, when a dominant mood is the desire to inspire fits of envy in one's friends, a woman (and sometimes a man) in the role of arm candy expresses the quintessential modern relationship. It's a one-night thing, a post-sexual image enhancer and ego booster. In the conventional pairing—powerful older man, stunning young woman—her presence assures the seething jealousy of other men and guarantees the intrigued interest of women."

—Kuczynski 1998, p. 9.1

tions at all levels—heterogender. Heterogender differentiation will not disappear or change until a transformation in its organizing institution—heterosexuality, and the interests it serves—occurs.

"Movies, the fashion industry, magazines and television have discovered that weddings sell" (Spindler 1998, 9.1). But more than that, they've discovered that we'll consent. In order to give consent, one must be assured that there will be certain rewards. One of the central ways they succeed is by convincing consumers that romance is both necessary and sacred and far outweighs the realities of the marketplace and its consequences for consumers, labor, communities, social groups, and countries.

In order for the wedding industry to be "recession-proof"—that is, that people will pay for a wedding no matter what—it must rely on a very powerful meaning-making apparatus guaranteeing our compliance and consent to participate. This *wedding-ideological complex* is made up of those sites in American popular culture—children's toys, wedding announcements, advertising, film, television, bridal magazines, jokes, cartoons, music—that *work as an ensemble in creating many taken-for-granted beliefs, values, and assumptions within social texts and practices about weddings.* One of the central functions of this complex is to create the conditions that allow us to imagine possibilities in relation to weddings, marriage, and heterosexuality. The beliefs we hold about weddings and marriage emanate from a variety of historical and material sites and are made use of daily in the wedding market. These meanings rely on romantic and sacred notions of heterosexuality in order to create and maintain the illusion of well-being—the heterosexual imaginary. This romantic view of weddings, marriage, and heterosexuality prevents us from seeing the powerful arrangements these meanings serve as well as the consequences they produce.

The prevailing national and state interests of this historical moment are those of transnational capitalist patriarchy. But what does that mean in terms of our everyday lives? In part it means we live in a country that is highly stratified: where the rich control most of the income and wealth, consume the largest amount of goods and services, receive the highest quality schooling, and enjoy the best health care money can buy and where men and whites are privileged.

What does this have to do with the portrayal of weddings in popular culture? In recent years we have been watching the rich get richer and the poor get poorer. In fact, as of 1993, the richest 20 percent of American families earned 46.8 percent of all available income and controlled 80 percent of the country's wealth—stocks, bonds, real estate, and other private property. The wealthiest 5 percent of families "control more than half the nation's property" (Macionis 1997, 263). If 20 percent of the population controls 80 percent of the wealth and resources, that leaves the rest to be divided up among the remaining 80 percent of the population.

As you can see from Table 3.2, the rich control significant portions of the country's income and wealth, leaving the remainder to be divided among the lower classes. Given that much of the lower classes' income and wealth comes from the labor of those working *for* the richest 20 percent, it is the role of capitalist institutions and ideologies to justify this economic distribution and to gain the consent of the lower classes to participate in these arrangements. One of the dominant ideologies of capitalism, disseminated through a wide variety of institutions (e.g., education, law, media, family, government, and religion), is the belief that inequalities of wealth and income are socially just. In other words, to legitimize the concentration of wealth and income among a small number of Americans and to

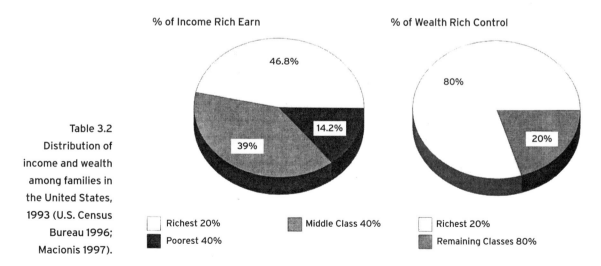

Table 3.2 Distribution of income and wealth among families in the United States, 1993 (U.S. Census Bureau 1996; Macionis 1997).

determine how the remainder will be distributed among the masses, ways of thinking about difference and value are necessary.

Competition, another central organizing principle of capitalism, combined with meaning-making systems circulating in an array of social practices including weddings, sets the terms for consenting to the ruling order and to its mechanisms for distributing what's left over. This is the primary rationale for belief systems organizing heterosexuality, race, class, gender, and age. Popular culture plays a crucial role in this regard by both justifying the dominant social order and binding us to it. As John Storey explains in his summary of Althusser's theory of ideology, prevailing rituals and customs

> offer pleasure and release from the usual demands of the social order, but . . . ultimately, they return us to our places in the social order, refreshed and ready to put up with our exploitation and oppression until the next *official* break comes along. In this sense ideology works to *reproduce* the social conditions and social relations necessary for the economic conditions and economic relations of capitalism to continue. (Storey 1993, 5)

The role of popular culture, and of weddings within that setting, is to provide that "official break." French sociologist Pierre Bourdieu further elaborates on this idea by linking cultural distinctions with class distinctions. Notions of style and taste become markers of class and status, "predisposed, consciously and deliberately or not, to fulfill a social function of legitimating social differences" (Bourdieu 1984, 5).

Popular culture, which is also mass culture and dominated by the mass media—television, film, magazines, newspapers, radio, and the Internet—is controlled by the same owning class that controls the country's wealth and income. Six major corporations control most of America's media: General Electric (NBC), Disney (ABC), Westinghouse (CBS), Turner Broadcasting (TBS), Rupert Murdoch (Fox), and Time Warner (TNT). Consequently, their role in ruling and the production of meaning is also significant. The next two chapters will focus on the meaning-mak-

"The richest fifth of the world's people consumes 86 percent of all goods and services while the poorest fifth consumes just 1.3 percent. Indeed, the richest fifth consumes 45 percent of all meat and fish, 58 percent of all energy used and 84 percent of all paper, has 74 percent of all telephone lines and owns 87 percent of all vehicles."

—Annan 1998, p. 16

"The three richest people in the world have assets that exceed the combined gross domestic product of the 48 least developed countries."

—Annan 1998, p. 16

ing processes of the wedding-ideological complex organizing the portrayal of weddings and the "recession-proof" wedding industry. Several sites within American popular culture will be examined for the ways they exploit utopian desires for community, love, and belonging by using the ideology of romantic love to secure particular class and race interests.

"Isn't It Romantic . . . ?"

One of the central organizing concepts of the wedding-ideological complex is the notion of romance or romantic love. But what is *romance* or *romantic love* and how do they work to organize how we think about weddings? To begin, romance is ideology in action. Ideology manifests in words and images, which establish and regulate the meanings and beliefs justifying dominant interests. Romance is not only applicable to love but can be applied to any area, e.g., sports, patriotism, and work.

In the instance of romantic love the focus is on what is commonly thought of as a private or personal emotion that mysteriously manifests as "chemistry," "a crush," or "falling in love." It is thought of as an unexplainable and natural emotion—as long as it's heterosexual—as opposed to one that is socially produced and organized. The ideology of romantic love is a belief in a social relation disconnected from real conditions of existence—a social relation that masks or conceals contradictions in favor of reproducing a reassuring illusion or the promise of well-being and bonding. This ideal depends upon a belief in monogamous coupling as the preferred manifestation of love relationships, making all other possibilities unimaginable or unacceptable. It also elevates the individuals in the couple to the status of unique and exclusive, bestowed with the mantle of "chosen one" or "one and only" from "now until forever," " 'til death do us part." It is here that the ideology of romantic love incorporates property relations, naturalizing love with ownership, a pervasive belief about romance, commitment, and marriage. The extension of these beliefs manifests in feelings of possessiveness, jealousy, and, in many cases, violence. In the words of the popular song "End of the Road," from Boyz II Men,

> Although we've come
> To the end of the road
> Still I can't let go
> It's unnatural
> You belong to me
> I belong to you.

Patriarchal heterosexuality makes use of the ideology of romantic love in the interests of male dominance and capitalism. It reinforces a heterogendered division of labor which subordinates women's needs to men's desires and is central to the heterosexual imaginary. Creating the illusion of plenitude and fullness, the ideology of romantic love produces a belief that sexual objectification and subordination is both natural and justified. Enormous inequities are overlooked when the promise of romance presents itself. And women are more subject to this outcome than men, given their positioning by the wedding-ideological complex. For example, from early childhood women are socialized to accept these practices and beliefs. The alienation from the real that this situation produces is significant, manifesting in responses to domestic violence—"but I love him"—to "falling in love" with the fantasy of romantic love as opposed to the real person.

The political spectacle of the Clinton-Lewinsky affair illustrates how this works. Consider this excerpt from the Starr Report, paraphrasing and sometimes quoting Ms. Lewinsky's description of her relationship with President Clinton:

> The President was the "most affectionate with me he'd ever been," Ms. Lewinsky testified. He stroked her arm, toyed with her hair, kissed her neck, praised her intellect and beauty. . . . He remarked . . . that he wished he had more time for me. And so I said, well, maybe you will have more time in three years. And I was . . . thinking just when he wasn't President, he was going to have more time on his hands. And he said, well, I don't know, I might be alone in three years. And then I said something about . . . us sort of being together. I think I kind of said, oh, I think we'd be a good team, or something like that. . . . [he responded

with a reference to being significantly older than her] "I left that day
sort of emotionally stunned," for "I just knew he was in love with me."
(Starr Report 1998)

In this passage the ideology of romantic love is evident in Lewinsky's translation of a moment of affection intended to romance the ending of their relationship into her fantasy of a lifelong romantic bond. Lewinsky's fetishizing of the President works to obscure the enormous complexities and contradictions of an extramarital affair between the most powerful man in the world and an intern, a fifty-year-old and a twenty-year-old, in the context of a significant political struggle for control of the White House. More reminiscent of fairy tales or romance novels, this story exemplifies the crises romantic mythologies yield when confronted with reality. As Nicola Field argues in her theory of romance, "The ideology of romance overrides contradictions and simplifies overwhelming complexities. Romance is there to blur the past, and fudge over the real contradictions of the present, in order to control the future" (Field 1995, 29). In a satirical article in the *New York Times Magazine* (on September 13, 1998) the Sunday after the Starr Report was released, the use of the white wedding to erase the taint of scandal is suggested. Titled "Miss Lewinsky: Are You Ready for Your Makeover Now?," this article offers three options for blurring the past and getting her "life back": "quiet respectability," "marrying well," and "questing for fame." Each recommendation is accompanied by a photo overlaid with a paperdoll outfit to exemplify the option being offered. The second choice, "marrying well," features Lewinsky in a wedding gown. Lisa Johnson, author of *How to Snare a Millionaire*, is quoted as recommending that Lewinsky "slim down at a Palm Springs spa, where she can 'learn the rich man's sports of tennis and golf under the tutelage of gorgeous foreign pros'" on her way to finding a wealthy man to marry her. After several tongue-in-cheek recommendations for associating with the upper class as a way to recuperate her reputation, this section quotes Geraldo Rivera as saying, "Monica will make the perfect trophy wife for the next millennium." Clearly, weddings certify more than whether a woman is "pretty enough."

In the wake of a similar scandal portrayed in the film *The Birdcage*, the senator's

"Diary"
"Looking for Love in the Feds Funds Rate."
Like a love-struck intern parsing the boss's every word for a sign that the feeling is mutual, world markets hunted obsessively last week for reasons to believe that the Federal Open Market Committee would cut interest rates at its meeting on Tuesday.
Hearts skipped beats at midweek when Alan Greenspan suggested to Congress that action was needed "shortly" to keep the contagion of economic instability now afflicting emerging markets from "really spilling over and creating some very significant further difficulties." The remark apparently sounded enough like "Will you marry me?" to send stocks soaring for a day. By week's end, the main question seemed to be how big a diamond, er, rate cut would be forthcoming.

—*New York Times* 1998, p. 3.4

wife recommends a high-status wedding for their daughter as a way to cleanse away the shame of the past. She exclaims,

> What about a wedding? A big white wedding! Why not? It would restore your image. A wedding is hope, a white wedding is *family and morality and tradition* and it would be such a special marriage . . . and to a cultural attaché's son. It would be *love and optimism versus cynicism and sex*!! It would be an affirmation!

These examples reflect the success of the wedding-ideological complex in guaranteeing future markets and preserving ruling-class interests by securing in the collective conscious the association of weddings with whiteness and wealth, morality and optimism. Whiteness, wealth, and weddings become central features of the ideology of romantic love, communicating a sign system that collapses them into one package. The way the heterosexual imaginary works is by making use of both fantasy and nostalgia. The effect is a masking of the very real, contradictory, and complicated ways institutionalized heterosexuality works in the interests of the dominant classes. Through the use of nostalgia, romance renarrates history and naturalizes tradition. Tradition, then, is left unquestioned, providing a vehicle for ruling-class interests to be both emulated and legitimized.

In a recent issue of *Bride's* a story called "Dangerous Liaisons: Rewriting History for Hollywood's Classic Couples," the magazine rewrites sad movie endings as "happily ever afters" to help the new bride imagine her marriage as a success.

> As you look forward to your own happily-ever-after, consider the fate of some of Hollywood's most famous lovers. . . . Devoted fans were left wondering "What if?" To give everyone closure, we've rewritten history for five beloved couples from both the small and silver screen. Because, frankly, we die-hard romantics still give a damn. (Toussaint 1997/1998, 421)

Following this introduction, *Bride's* goes on to rewrite endings for movies such as *The Way We Were*, *Casablanca*, *Star Wars*, and *Batman*, providing brides with messages about which romances *should* have failed and which should have been given another chance. *The Way We Were* ended properly, in that Katie and Hubbell divorced. They were a mismatch to start—but particularly because of Katie's "perfectionism" and "nagging." In the rewriting of *Casablanca*, Ilsa divorces her "boring husband," finds Rick, and marries him. Clearly, women like Ilsa deserve men like Rick, but "nagging" women don't earn a second chance. The message to new brides: exemplify the Ingrid Bergman type of femininity, be the good wife, and don't nag! It's your responsibility to make the marriage work!

This rewriting of Hollywood history provides a simulation of the celebrity wedding, using fairy tales as substitutes for the real. Once again the ideology of romantic love works to erase history in the interests of the illusion of heterosexual stability. Lessons on romance, romantic settings, and how to keep the romance alive work to secure the ideology of romantic love.

Brides and Barbies: Romancing the Clone

Central to the primary wedding market and to securing dominant class and race interests are bridal magazines. *Bride's* magazine, currently the largest magazine in the United States in terms of ad pages (seven hundred per issue), has a circulation of 405,000 per issue, is published six times per year, and costs $5 per copy. Their February/March 1998 issue was a record 1,150 pages. Owned by Newhouse Publications and controlled by Condé Nast-Advance Publications, *Bride's* is a key link in a corporation whose holdings include *Traveler*, which caters to honeymooners, *Allure, Glamour, Gourmet, GQ, House & Garden, Sports for Women, Vanity Fair, Vogue*, and numerous newspapers, textbook, and cable companies.

With the median age of newlyweds rising along with increases in higher education and career opportunities for women, *Bride's* recently changed its name to *Bride's and Your New Home*, adding regular sections on "Brides," "Weddings," "Honeymoon," and "Home." Given the average combined income of *Bride's* couples—$65,076 (*Bride's* 1997a), twice as affluent as the average U.S. household (at $35,492) (National Center for Health Statistics 1997)—advertisers recognize that they are primarily targeting both the owning class and the professional-managerial class (Ehrenreich 1989).

After thirty years as editor-in-chief, Barbara Tober recently retired from *Bride's* magazine. In an interview with the *Los Angeles Times,* Ms. Tober outlined her business philosophy. " ' When people marry, other people work. . . . A wedding brings economic health. . . . It is a great banquet from which everyone can derive a living. It makes enormous sense to me' " (Nibley 1994, D–7). *Bride's* has fashioned itself as the standard-bearer of wedding culture and as critical to a healthy economy. While many would characterize a magazine such as this as dealing only with the trivial in life, *Bride's* views its mission as stimulating the economy, providing jobs, and servicing newlyweds. In other words, it is aware of its role in attending to class interests, which it achieves through the romancing of heterosexuality.

The second leading bridal magazine is *Modern Bride.* Owned by Primedia Publications, *Modern Bride* publishes six issues per year, averaging 800 pages in length, at a cost of $5 per copy. Their circulation per issue is 371,294 readers. Similar to *Bride's, Modern Bride* has altered the sections of their magazine to provide broader coverage. Their magazine is divided into sections on "Cover Stories," "Fashion & Beauty," "Articles," "Home," and "Travel."

New entrants into the bridal magazine market include the rapidly growing Pace Communication's *Elegant Bride* (250 pages and 300,000 readers per issue), formerly *Southern Bride,* and Globe Communication's *Bridal Guide* (400 pages and 250,000 readers per issue), which also packages *Honeymoon Guide* and wedding catalogs with each issue. *For the Bride by Demetrios,* owned by Ilissa Bridals and published by DJE Publications, has also joined the pack with about 300 pages and a circulation of 160,000 per issue.

Other major magazines that feature special wedding issues include *Martha Stewart Living* and *Vogue. Living* is owned by Martha Stewart and published by Omni Media. She distributed two wedding issues in 1998 and will come out with four in 1999. Each magazine is about 300 pages in length and averages approximately 230,000 in circulation. What separates *Living* from the other magazines is that Stewart also features a "wedding week" on her daily television show to correspond with the publication of each wedding issue. Stewart is also the author of two wedding books—*The Wedding Planner* (1988) and *Weddings* (1987)—and is currently working on a third.

Bridal magazines
in a bookstore

Lesser known—and the only publication that caters to black brides—is *Signature Bride*. Privately owned by Deb Kronowitz and published four times a year by KLCS Communications, *Signature Bride* averages about 225 pages at a cost of $4 per issue. Its circulation is 75,000 and growing.

Seeing the enormous success of bridal magazines, many others have joined the market. Magazines such as *People, In Style, Star,* and *Town & Country* have all published special wedding issues. *Vogue* also published a special wedding issue in June 1998. Since their company also publishes *Bride's*, their features were primarily in keeping with *Vogue*'s fashion mission, with the brief but entertaining addition of a "Puppy Love" section featuring canine brides and grooms. There are also numerous regional wedding or bridal magazines such as *New England Bride's Wedding Guide, Cape Cod Wedding, New Jersey Weddings,* and others.

Book publishers have provided an onslaught of wedding guides. Most bookstores, regardless of size, feature a wedding section full of everything from etiquette guides to planners. Titles such as *Alternative Weddings, Weddings for Grown-Ups, Colin Cowie Weddings, Jumping the Broom, There Must Be Something for the Groom to Do, Weddings for Complicated Families, Wedding Plans,* and etiquette manuals from Emily Post and Amy Vanderbilt are regularly featured. Summer, the peak wedding season, is often a time when bookstores will display wedding books for interested customers. And, if this weren't enough, there is now wedding-planning software and a whole host of wedding websites where you can get advice on every feature of weddings, see what others have done, create your own site to share with friends and family, and even contract with or purchase various wedding services. (And this market is not even factored into the $32 billion annual revenues for weddings.)

Bridal magazines rely heavily on fairy-tale and storybook-romance themes in advertising, articles, and organization to sell everything one needs to produce their own wedding spectacle. As French theorist Guy Debord argues, the spectacle works symbolically. "The spectacle appears at once as society itself, as a part of society and as a means of unification. As a part of society, it is that sector where all attention, all consciousness, converges" (1994, 12). Examining bridal magazines for evidence of the role they play in the wedding industry and in the production of the wedding spectacle provides insight into the consciousness organizing these events. The images bridal magazines present distort reality and unify particular beliefs about heterosexuality, race, class, and gender. In *Bridal Gown Guide* (1998), Denise and Alan Fields offer an observation about bridal magazines and race:

> Only white people get married. Well, the major bridal magazines would
> never *say* that, but just take a look at the pictures. Page after page of
> Caucasian, size 8 models in $2,000 dresses. Just try to find a bride
> who's black, Hispanic or Asian. Go ahead, take as long as you need to

search. While you're at it, try to discover an ad that features a bride
who's a size 22. (15)

Three such industry distortions are revealed by this quote: race, class, and body
size. To verify this assertion by Denise and Alan Fields, I conducted an in-depth
study of the flagship of all bridal magazines, *Bride's,* and reviewed a number of
other regularly published national bridal magazines: *Modern Bride, Elegant Bride,
Bridal Guide, For the Bride by Demetrios,* and *Signature Bride.*

For *Bride's,* I visited the magazine archive at Condé Nast headquarters in New
York City and surveyed every issue from 1959, when Newhouse purchased the 25-
year-old magazine, to August/September 1998. Several interesting patterns were
evident, including verification of what the Fieldses asserted about race. Since 1959,
only four covers had women of color as the cover brides. The more typical cover representation was that of the thin, white, fair-haired—usually blond—blue-eyed young
woman. The first woman of color bridesmaid appeared in August 1972 on page
165. In the February/March 1976 issue, the first African-American bride was featured in an article, and in April/May 1977 the first black wedding party was displayed, on page 135.

Inside the magazine the representation of women of color varied depending upon
prominent events in a particular historical period. For example, from 1959 to the
late 1960s the magazine was completely white and made use of signifiers such as
"empire," "princess," and "royalty" in relation to anything bridal. The magazine's
primary focus was on the new wife and her domestic responsibilities, i.e., cooking.

During the late 1960s through the 1970s the magazine nearly disappeared. Marriage was extremely unpopular in these years as the "free love" movement and feminism asserted that it was a form of female servitude and male exploitation of
women. For the first time, *Bride's* offered advice on relationships, sexuality, and
on how to balance career and "wifestyle." The Vietnam War was an issue in feature articles on advice to brides. "How to" articles were present for brides planning
a wedding when their fiancé could be drafted. With the civil rights movement at a
peak during this same period, an increase in the visibility of African Americans
occurred.

By fall 1976, *Bride's* announced that "Romance is Back" and boldly referred to divorce on their cover. With the return of romance and the beginning of the Reagan era, the magazine thrived once again. The Reagan revolution of the 1980s and the myth of national prosperity as well as Diana and Charles's wedding in 1981 provided the backdrop for a significant increase in the size, quality, cost, and representations of expensive, upscale weddings. Work disappeared as a central topic and the magazine abounded with messages about "joy," "verve," "fun," "happiness," and "romance." As these markers of class interest increased, inclusion of women of color nearly disappeared again.

In the early 90s, the national trend toward multiculturalism and ethnic ambiguity coincided with a significant increase in the number of women of color from a range of ethnic groups in each issue of the magazine. While the presence of women of color is greater today than ever in the history of *Bride's* magazine, the numbers are still extremely low. Since 1990, the average percentage of black brides per issue in *Bride's* is 2.4 percent. This figure does not include women of color models who are of Latina, Asian, or Middle Eastern descent. With the dominant trend toward using light-skinned models, it is often difficult to ascertain if a bride is from one of these groups. Women of Asian descent are slightly easier to identify but are rarely used. The dominant icon of beauty, the white bride with blond hair, however, has averaged 30.7 percent of each issue during the 1990s.

While a small percentage of black brides are used in *Bride's* advertising, at least two to three times as many black women are used to advertise bridesmaids' dresses. In collecting these data, it was noticeable that no black bridesmaid appeared until after an average of one hundred and twenty white bridesmaids had appeared, a back-of-the-magazine phenomena for both black brides and bridesmaids. In one issue with few black brides, a photo spread in the rear of the magazine featured several large-size bride models; at least 50 percent of those represented were black women. As for bridesmaids, in the 1990s the number of blacks was two to three times greater than that of black brides, raising the question whether the phrase "Always a bridesmaid, never a bride" was really meant for black women. Or is it that the stereotype concerning who qualifies to be married excludes black women? One is left to wonder if the editors work to preserve the whiteness of this maga-

zine by assigning black women to the later pages as a way to preserve the race and class base of their readers.

In examining the other national bridal magazines, similar patterns appear. Except for *Signature Bride*, which targets African Americans, *all* the other magazines foreground white women as both brides and bridesmaids. Generally, black women don't appear in bridal magazines until at least halfway into each issue, and portrayals of bridal parties typically feature one black bridesmaid in a wedding party made up of several white women. For those brief displays of tuxedos for grooms, the same pattern holds true in that the groom is usually white with one black usher in the wedding party. Rarely do any of the bridal magazines feature predominantly black, hispanic, or Asian weddings and wedding parties with one or two whites. Consistent with this pattern, nonwhite weddings are almost never portrayed.

As mentioned earlier *Bride's* shifted its emphasis in the early 1990s by retitling their magazine *Bride's and Your New Home*. Now each issue includes an entire section on "the home." As the trendsetter for bridal magazines nationally, *Bride's* set the standard for most of the other leading bridal magazines, which now also include sections on gifts for the home, interior decorating, or home purchasing and repair. The assumption these magazines are designed around is that their primary market is middle- to upper-class, readers who have the desire and means to own a home. This change in format, combined with the racialized patterns of representation in bridal gown ads, suggests that the intentionally or unintentionally targeted wedding market for bridal magazines is white, middle- to upper-class, and propertied.

The dominant image of Mattel's Barbie doll is similar to that used in bridal magazines. Historically, Barbie and her corresponding Bridal Barbie are white, blond, blue-eyed, thin, and "pretty." Contrasted against the images in *Bride's*, model, real, and toy brides all seem to look alike, sending the message that to be a bride is to look this way, to buy these products, and to participate in a heterogendered, racial, and class division of labor in keeping with these images.

The packages containing the bridal gowns for dressing Barbie all feature ads on the back of the carton. Four dolls appear in these ads, illustrating the range of

"Each pale yellow wrapper has a picture on it. A picture of little Mary Jane, for whom the candy is named. Smiling white face. Blond hair in gentle disarray, blue eyes looking at her out of a world of clean comfort. They eyes are petulant, mischievous. To Pecola they are simply pretty. She eats the candy, and its sweetness is good. To eat the candy is somehow to eat the eyes, eat Mary Jane. Love Mary Jane. Be Mary Jane."

—Morrison 1970, p. 43

Girl dressed as
Barbie bride for
Halloween

Bridal doll in
store window

options available for dressing Barbie. Three of the featured dolls are light-haired, white, and blue-or green-eyed, and each is dressed in a white bridal gown. The fourth, a brunette with brown eyes, is wearing a bridesmaid's gown, repeating the ethnic distribution pattern seen in the bridal magazines.

Marketed to 4- to 7-year-old girls, the "My Size Bride Barbie" mentioned earlier is clad in a white wedding gown that can be worn by the child who owns the doll. Little girls of all races get to dress like Barbie and imagine themselves as white, blond, thin, and pretty Barbie, even if they don't fit into any of these categories. Barbie products, which are wildly popular with young girls, teach children many powerful messages, the least of which is what race is the most important. While Mattel offers a range of "multicultural" Barbies, there is little variation in the facial or body characteristics of these multiethnic dolls, and the default Barbie is still understood to be white. The effect is that these products and bridal magazine marketing privilege middle-class whites. For children of color, the message is one of assimilation. Considered in relation to the images portrayed in bridal magazines, the expectation that women of color emulate white women is clearly reinforced. As bell hooks argues in her essay "Overcoming White Supremacy," "Assimilation has provided social legitimation for this shift in allegiance. It is a strategy deeply rooted in the ideology of white supremacy, as its advocates urge black people to negate blackness and imitate whites" (1990, 24). Mattel, Disney, Hasbro, and other toy companies market a variety of children's products that feature the same dominant images of the pretty white bride whose greatest achievement is in wedding her handsome prince. The wedding becomes both the object of a young girl's dreams and the site of closure, rendering the marital relationship invisible.

Women's experience with weddings and the wedding industry is racially structured. Over and over again the icon of the beautiful white bride in the beautiful white bridal gown is replayed and reinforced, sending a clear message to young and old alike that what counts as beautiful and marriageable is white. Not only does this process secure the consent of white women in participating in the commodification of weddings, but it also contributes to the production of white heterosexual privilege.

In fall 1998, President Clinton's Initiative on Race resulted in an assessment of American attitudes and practices that reinforce white privilege. In the summary report, the committee concluded that Americans need to be educated about " 'white privilege' and how it disenfranchises every group that came here without it" (Ross 1997, 1). Both the primary and secondary wedding markets are rife with instances in which "whites tend to benefit, either unknowingly or consciously, from this country's history of white privilege" (1).

"Fairy Tales Can Come True, It Can Happen to You . . ."

In bridal magazines and in children's toys, references to fairy tales and princesses dominate, although less so today than in the 1980s. In bridal magazines since the 1950s, advertisements have frequently made reference to the bride as "princess," "royalty," or as having an "empire." Along with the demise of the British Empire, colonial references have also disappeared, but the ideology of romantic love linked to fairy tales and princesses still prevails. Children still pretend to be princesses waiting for their handsome prince to arrive, the story of Cinderella continues to be popular, and Cinderella themes still echo through the wedding market. Even "My Size Bride Barbie" also comes in "My Size Princess Barbie." And, with the exception of the 1997 release of Disney's multicultural *Cinderella* movie, produced by Whitney Houston, all the instances of brides and princesses in children's culture are white.

In the past few years, bridal gown advertisers have abandoned the use of captions and have, instead, relied upon elegant settings and luxurious accessories such as diamond tiaras to signify princess bride and couture. Princess Diana's reputation with couture designs is most noticeable in the linkage of romance to class through references to "couture" in bridal gown advertising, e.g., Jim Hjelm Couture Collection, Carol Hai Designs, and Carmi Couture Collection. By allowing brides to imagine themselves as having access to high-fashion and "couture" gowns, advertisers create the perception that there is little difference between the average bride and the princess bride. "Style" becomes something disconnected from class and wealth and thus available to most women, regardless of income. One effect of this practice is that most women spend beyond their means to purchase their dream gown. They can't even imagine getting married without one.

When these patterns are considered in relation to the history of marriage, the interests served by weddings and marriage have not changed much. Throughout the history of Western marriage, certain groups have been excluded from participation. As a property-based relation established for the protection of wealth, the creation of heirs, and the reproduction of the division of labor, certain groups did not qualify. For example, in some locations in medieval Europe, the poor were not allowed to marry (Mies 1986). It was a practice reserved for the propertied classes, and in some cases only for the royal family. Not until the rich realized the need for the reproduction of working-class labor were the poor allowed to marry.

In colonial America, marriage was also a patriarchal arrangement, with fathers regarded as the head of the family and women and children part of his property holdings. Unpropertied whites and free blacks could marry, but they were still under the rule of the propertied class. "Although unmarried women had the right to own property, enter into contracts, and represent themselves in court, after marriage the English concept of coverture was evoked, whereby the wife's legal identity was subsumed in that of her husband, giving him the authority to make decisions for her" (Schwartz and Scott 1997, 13).

White slave owners did not allow African slaves in the United States and the Caribbean to "legally" marry. This right was reserved for whites and was linked to both white supremacy and the passing of property from father to son. In the following passage, bell hooks describes the relationship of marriage to assimilation practices where blacks imitated whites:

> As the displaced African assimilated American values, they wanted to have the ecclesiastical and civil ceremonies their masters and mistresses had; they desired public acknowledgment of their union. Although there were never any legally acknowledged marriages between slaves, they wanted the same marriage rituals their white owners enacted. (hooks 1981, 43)

As a way to effect a symbolic union similar to marriage, African slaves from a variety of African cultures combined their knowledge to create new rituals. The significance of brooms and of sticks in various African cultures combined with the once-popular ritual among white American colonists of holding hands and jumping over a broom to make the practice of "jumping the broom" a ritual sanctioned by some white plantation owners who allowed African slave marriages. Even though some slave owners permitted a marriage ritual, it was not legally binding and could be dissolved at the master's request (Cole 1995; hooks 1981; Stevenson 1996).

"The most common type of heterosexual marriage in all Mediterranean societies (and the only legal form at Athens and Rome) was monogamy: a male-female couple. Such unions were often officially possible only for the properties classes, but the monogamous permanent relationships of the lower classes were apparently understood as analagous."

—Boswell 1994, p. 32

With the emergence of capitalism, these images have shifted according to the needs of the marketplace and the division of labor. With this history, it's not surprising to see the emphasis placed on wealth and accumulation in today's wedding industry, effectively putting the traditional white wedding out of reach particularly for the poor, even though they might make every effort to locate a wedding gown that would allow them to "fit" with dominant cultural depictions of the "legitimate" white wedding. To accommodate this need, even thrift stores provide significant offerings for potential brides.

"Thank Heaven for Little Girls . . . "

The cultural codes of traditional femininity permeate bridal culture, from Barbie and other wedding toys to messages in bridal advertising, even though marketers are aware that they are catering to women who occupy positions of privilege and power. Many women have commented in bridal magazines and other sites that even though they typically don't participate in traditionally feminine behavior, they will deviate from this norm in order to have the wedding they've been imagining and preparing for since they were children. While the trend in bridal gown advertising has been toward the marketing of the couture dress, many gown-sellers rely on codes of femininity to attract a buyer. For example, David's Bridal, the discount gown outlet, runs a twenty-page ad highlighting little girls and grown-up brides. David's ads begin with a page of flower girls with the caption "Thank heaven for little girls . . . " followed by a corresponding page of adult brides with the text, "They grow up in the most delightful ways." These messages portray the bride as feminine, innocent, child-like, and youthful. It is commonplace in these ads to see reference to childhood dreams and desires. Listed below are some of the messages David's Bridal uses:

> "Sugar and spice and everything nice"
> "Girlish charm knows no boundaries"
> "From innocence of child to the radiance of a bride"
> "Playing dress-up was never like this"

"Little girls aren't the only ones who love pink"

"As soft as your first teddy bear, as tender as your first kiss"

"Girls just want to have fun"

The ideal of femininity reproduced in these quotes reflects middle-class standards for "appropriate" heterogendered behavior, resecuring women's role as subordinate to men.

In a racialized context, such as that of bridal magazines or wedding toys, this standard also reflects white interests. Sociologist Rose Brewer theorizes the race, class, gender connection by demonstrating the ways these categories benefit the "white power elite":

> Cultural practice, beliefs and ideology also structure female labor. The ideology of what is appropriately Black women's work is played out in the arena of the public social reproduction of labor. Kitchen and cafeteria workers, nurses' aides: these are defined as appropriate jobs for Black women, very much as the domestic labor of a generation ago was defined as "Black women's work." (Brewer 1997, 27)

The images of femininity and whiteness that so pervade popular cultural sites serve to secure in the collective imagination the place of women from particular classes and racial groups. It's much easier to imagine a black, working-class woman as a token collector in the New York subway system than it is to imagine a white, middle- to upper-class woman who is as "soft as her teddy bear" and full of "sugar and spice." The absence of women of color from popular cultural sites does as much to reproduce racialized relations of production as the presence of white women as classic brides.

In addition to securing class interests in relation to labor, these images play a key role in establishing patterns of social reproduction. Signifiers of femininity vary from class to class because women in each class have different responsibilities for socializing their families to take their "place" in capitalist patriarchy. For example, feminine training for children from the professional-managerial class is significantly different than for children from the working or middle classes. Barbie is a classic example of this. While she can be a mother, a wife, a hair dresser, and a makeup artist, she can also venture out of her class, albeit briefly, to be a veterinarian—all the while maintaining her femininity, never in doubt, as the hypercompensating pink that marks all Barbie products reminds us. The roles "allowed" for Barbie don't cross over into upper-class or professional-managerial practices. (There is no "Debutante Barbie" or "CEO Barbie.") Barbie will most likely grow up to marry, have a house, be a homemaker and mother, and be skilled to do the work of raising children like herself. Verena Stolcke's succinct analysis of this process sees this as an issue of social control:

> [While] class oppression and the social division of labour have their origins in unequal access to the means of production, it is social reproduction, i.e., the perpetuation of class relations and domination—mediated directly by the institution of marriage, the family and inheritance—which requires (and thus determines) both women's primary assignment to domestic labour and the undervaluation of this function. . . . [T]he social control of women through marriage differs by class and has different implications for economic roles in different classes. (1983, 163)

While marriage is not specific to capitalism, the particular way it is organized through rules of conduct and inheritance is reinforced by the wedding industry, particularly in relation to the accumulation of property. This is where monogamous marriage is critical to capitalism and patriarchy; it secures women's subordination to men, preserves heirs, ensures that property passes within the family, and maintains class supremacy. Even biblical definitions of adultery reflect the historical need to know who fathered a child. Leviticus 20:10 identifies adulterous behavior as sexual intercourse with another man's wife. It does not specify that an adulterous man also be married, since the violation is of another man's property—the wife—and claims to fatherhood (heirs).

While many people subscribe to broader interpretations of adultery, this histo-

An example of weddings as a media priority

ry of patriarchal interests still informs today's practices. For example, social sanctions against married women who "stray" are more severe than for men. Women who don't comply with dominant monogamous marriage are far more threatening to the dominant social order than are men who marry and engage in extra-marital affairs. In a recent article in the *New York Times*, Gustav Niebuhr discusses the role of women in relation to monogamous marriage:

> As the magisterial *Anchor Bible Dictionary* (1992) puts it, the man's marital status was "inconsequential since only the married or betrothed woman" was "bound to fidelity." The prohibition was not so much about a husband's feelings as about knowing who had fathered a baby. Thus, it worked to safeguard issues of family succession and property rights. (1998, 5)

The history of the wedding ring is rooted in these understandings as well. Even today, only the bride is "required" to wear a wedding ring, signifying her monogamous bond to the husband. Historically grooms weren't required to wear a wedding ring. While this has become more common, it is still optional for men.

Creating the idealized notion of monogamous marriage is one of the central roles of the heterosexual imaginary. The wedding industry and its wedding-ideological complex display images that secure women's consent to participate in these arrangements.

The Spectacle of Accumulation

A Macy's ad in *Bride's* magazine proclaims, "You're getting married, you want the whole world to know." But why? What is the appeal of this public display?

American institutions and popular culture begin preparing women from childhood for their eventual role as the center of attraction and producer of the public wedding spectacle. Over and over again women proclaim they've been waiting for this moment since they were young children. Barbie dolls with bridal gowns and bridal parties, "My Size Bride Barbie," which allows girls to try on the wedding gown, Disney films, television cartoons and sitcoms, soap operas, messages from family members, roles as flower girls and junior bridesmaids, and wedding toys that invite little girls to plan a pretend wedding all contribute to this effort.

Popular culture plays a central role in producing the desire for a big white wedding extravaganza. In addition to bridal magazines, celebrity magazines such as *People, In Style,* and *Jet* and the *Sunday New York Times* wedding pages participate in the wedding-ideological complex.

Bridal magazines make it their business to prepare the bride for her part in "the most important day of her life" and for planning "her day." Using slogans such as these is common throughout bridal literature. By producing and exploiting the bride's well-developed fantasy of the "perfect" wedding with her as the "perfect" bride with the "perfect" romance, the wedding industry is able to promote accumulation. Everything—from advice on cosmetics to planning and timetable checklists—is provided. Headlines such as "Create the most romantic wedding ever: Brilliant bouquets, Storybook sites, and details that make a difference," "20 gorgeous hair ideas," or "Princess Diana—Her wedding remembered" offer advice and fodder for the imagination.

Displayed as the exemplar of the ultimate wedding, Princess Diana's ceremony helps the new bride imagine her own, inviting her to emulate and legitimize upper-class practices, as though the average middle-class bride could ever achieve anything remotely similar to this pageant. While the "how-to" columns provide brides-to-be with information in planning their wedding and choosing their wedding gown, one of the most important roles bridal magazines play is in capturing the bride-to-be's imagination. Real wedding stories about celebrities support advertisers' efforts to reach their audience, secure the economic health of bridal magazines, and ensure that the consumption-based wedding market imagines itself emulating royalty and wealth.

As part of the wedding-ideological complex, media constructions of celebrity weddings play a powerful part in linking romance with accumulation. Represented as the "real," celebrity weddings appeal to readers as actual manifestations of the fairy-tale or storybook romance.

Princess Diana's wedding, the most retold of all celebrity weddings, serves as

Mary to Tyrone: "Do you remember our wedding, dear? I'm sure you've completely forgotten what my wedding gown looked like. Men don't notice such things. They don't think they're important. But it was important to me, I can tell you! . . .

Where is my wedding gown now, I wonder? I kept it wrapped up in tissue paper in my trunk. I used to hope I would have a daughter and when it came time for her to marry—She couldn't have bought a lovelier gown. . . . It was made of soft, shimmering satin, trimmed with wonderful old duchesse lace, in tiny ruffles around the neck and sleeves, and worked in with the folds that were draped round in a bustle effect at the back. The basque was boned and very tight. I remember I held my breath when it was fitted, so my waist would be as small as possible. . . . Oh how I loved that gown! It was so beautiful! Where is it now, I wonder? I used to take it out from time to time when I was lonely. . . ."

—Eugene O'Neill,
*Long Day's Journey
Into Night*

the ideal. In recognition of the one-year anniversary of her death in 1997, numerous television networks aired video footage of Diana's and Charles's wedding, *Bride's* magazine offered a retrospective, and *People* put out a special issue called *Unforgettable Women of the Century* with a small photo of Diana in her wedding tiara featured on the cover next to the other princess bride, Princess Grace, displayed prominently in the center of the cover.

MSNBC's *Time & Again* replayed Prince Charles's and Lady Diana's wedding telecast, complete with narration from then and now. Jane Paulie and Tom Brokaw were the co-anchors on July 29, 1981, who provided commentary for this momentous occasion. Jane Paulie referred to this as "the day [Diana] became a wife and a princess." Tom Brokaw certified the importance and size of the royal spectacle by mentioning that 750 million people, according to BBC estimates, in sixty-one countries would be viewing the event. Descriptions from both Paulie and Brokaw alternated between fascination with Charles's and Diana's romance and amazement at their wealth. Brokaw reported that the wedding presents "have been presided over by none less than a rear admiral." He commented on two of the gifts, a $20,000 fully equipped kitchen, "which they accepted," and a special bed named for Lady Diana. The bed was made with twelve hundred springs, which, according to the bed maker, were useful "just in case [Charles] comes home late so she won't be disturbed."

Jane Paulie commented on Diana's demeanor during the ceremony as "bride's sweet timidity . . . [in this] utterly traditional twentieth-century wedding." Of course, Paulie had no idea if, in fact, the bride was feeling timid, but read these classic codes of femininity into what she perceived as a feminine event.

As the ceremony began Brokaw exclaimed that soon the "glass coach bearing Lady Diana" would appear. What did appear didn't seem to be glass but was a black and gold coach with coachmen dressed in full red and gold uniforms with tri-point hats of black and gold. While the carriage was extremely ornate and expensive, the idea of a "glass coach" called up images of Cinderella and fairy tales.

Both commentators were very concerned with what appeared to be a lack of romantic display following the ceremony. Paulie kept commenting on how she was waiting for Charles to look into Diana's face as a signifier of their romantic bond. Both Brokaw and Paulie repeatedly referred to this and waited for some public display of affection which could be construed as romance. Finally, from the balcony of Buckingham Palace, Diana and Charles looked into each other's faces and smiled. Brokaw and Paulie were gratified.

In keeping with the tenets of patriarchal religious ceremonies, the presiding clergy outlined what marriage is, proclaiming it to be "an honorable estate . . . signifying the mystical union between Christ and his church." He also offered three reasons why marriage is important: 1) for the "increase of mankind" where children will be brought up in "fear and nurture of the Lord"; 2) to honor the "natural instincts and affections implanted by God" which should be "hallowed by God"; and 3) to serve the interests of "mutual society, health and comfort in prosperity and adversity." After reciting these religious ideological messages concerning marriage, the priest asked, "Who gives this woman to this man?" At that point, Lady Diana's father literally gave Diana's hand to Prince Charles. Charles then placed a ring on Diana's finger and did not receive one for himself. This striking display of patriarchal tradition resecures the upper-class role of Princess Diana as wife, future mother, and future queen. This act of placing her hand into Charles's so that the ring can be placed there boldly demonstrates the transference of daughter as property of the father to husband as the new proprietor, signified by the wedding ring. Her labor will serve the interests of the British crown in providing heirs and in socializing them appropriately for their life as royalty.

This display reflects a powerful relationship among romance, religious ideology, property, and wealth or accumulation. The spectacle of wealth is never called into question but is, instead, romanticized by the emcees. The conditions upon which any of these vast holdings have been amassed are rendered invisible by the heterosexual imaginary that collapses the romantic and the material world together.

In his book *Society of the Spectacle*, Guy Debord discusses the role of celebrities in the production of the spectacle:

> Media stars are spectacular representations of living human beings,
> distilling the essence of the spectacle's banality into images of possible

> roles. Stardom is a diversification in the semblance of life—the object of
> an identification with mere appearance which is intended to
> compensate for the crumbling of directly experienced . . . activity.
> (1994, 38)

The spectacle—especially the media or celebrity spectacle—works ideologically, conveying to the observer/reader what they *should* believe about romance, weddings, marriage, and heterosexuality. Celebrity spectacles become the vehicles through which the masses not only imagine the possibility of wealth and fame but seek to emulate it as well, thereby legitimating the accumulation practices of the rich and famous.

People magazine's annual special issues on celebrity weddings as well as their ongoing reporting teach us not only what counts as celebrity but also the importance of romance and the wedding in American society. To qualify for a wedding announcement in *People*, one must be either famous or notorious. Included in their coverage are royalty, celebrated and successful athletes, athletes who have fallen from grace and have been "saved" by marriage, film, television, and theater stars, politicians and those who have had affairs with politicians, and music celebrities.

The reporting of celebrity weddings follows many of the same patterns visible in the presentation of Princess Diana's wedding. Of course, central to all of the coverage, regardless of status, ethnicity, or religion, is the image of the bride in her white wedding gown. Except for a couple of notable and predictable exceptions—Roseanne, for instance, marries in red—the vast majority of celebrity weddings feature a white bride with a white wedding gown. Periodicals that serve predominantly black, hispanic, native, or Asian audiences feature women of color as brides, also clad in white wedding gowns. Even when one wedding took place in Shanghai, the bride still wore white.

Evidence of accumulation is also present in the reporting of celebrity weddings. While some weddings are certainly small and simple, the vast majority are sites for spectacular display. For instance, Gina Marie Tolleson rode to her wedding in a white carriage drawn by a white horse to marry Alan Thicke. Céline Dion needed a "month to plan" her hairdo and "1,000 hours to make her pearl-encrusted gown." Wed in Notre Dame Basilica in Montreal, Dion and her groom René Angélil had some nine hundred people "working for [their] wedding to happen." Emulating the attire of a queen, Dion wore a tiara that weighed twenty pounds.

People magazine's wedding annuals are extraordinarily popular among readers. They are filled with photographs and brief descriptions of weddings. The format they use for reporting these events fits with the notion of media star as spectacle and foregrounds the exceptional about these events. All descriptions include ages of the bride and groom. Interestingly, when someone refuses to give their age, *People* comments on this noncompliance. Of course, we're left wondering why the ages of the newlyweds are significant for these reports.

While the vast majority marry people of similar ages, the effect is that significant age differences are more noticeable. In a section called "Wedding Shockers," *People* offers the equivalent of the wedding freak show, highlighting those marriages that break from the norm. In 1995 they focused their attention on the Michael Jackson–Lisa Marie Presley wedding and contrasted it with Jerry Lee Lewis's marriage to an eighth-grader in 1957, suggesting by association that both marriages were deviant. Most significant of those listed in this section was the wedding of Guess model Anna Nicole Smith, 27, to J. Howard Marshall II, 90.

> "I'm very much in love," Smith told an interviewer, flashing her asteroid-size 22-carat engagement diamond and her diamond-dusted wedding band.... "I could have married him four years ago if I'd just wanted to get rich...." His mistress of 10 years during his second marriage was a flamboyant Texas socialite named "Lady" Walker. (She died while undergoing cosmetic surgery in 1991.) (*People* 1995b, 125)

The effect of reports like these is heteronormative. Stories of the unusual or the odd serve to secure the "normal," the center, making all who occupy this space feel comforted by their compliance.

Another pattern prevalent in these wedding reports is that of listing the celebrity guests. The effect is to both certify the celebrity and to provide an imaginary sense of the consolidation of wealth and fame by revealing privileged circles of friends and associates. The greater the listing of celebrities, the more spectacular the wedding.

One aspect of celebrity weddings that has become normative is the presence of children. About 45 percent of the couples listed in these issues have been married before, had children from a previous relationship, or had been living together for several years and already had children. Several brides were pregnant at the time of the wedding and some insisted on getting married so that they could have children. In one article in *People*, the writer asserts that the birth of a child becomes the impetus for celebrities to marry and sometimes symbolically replaces the engagement ring. "These days . . . a pregnancy is tantamount to a diamond. . . . When couples have children, the child is a sign of commitment." (*People* 1997, 169).

While nationally the social trend is away from thinking of children conceived outside of marriage as "illegitimate," the history of this stigma remains, especially for the poor. For the conservative right and among many politicians, the call for family values is frequently code for "nuclear family," where the children are raised in a two-parent, patriarchal, heterosexual, married household. This ideological position formed the foundation of the marriage campaign embedded within the recent welfare reform legislation passed by the U.S. Congress. While these groups reject the possibility that children can be raised in a healthy, loving, and growthful environment that does not fit this model, the reality is quite the contrary. The relevance of the nuclear family model is rapidly waning, returning us to a model more similar to the pre-World War II family (Coontz 1997).

Many people generally believe it is "necessary" to marry when there are children involved. Marriage becomes the way to certify legitimacy, normalcy, and morality. The heterosexual imaginary circulating here prevents people from seeing the role of marriage in preserving heirs and protecting private property. It also conceals from view the various abuses outlined in Chapter 2 and the ways weddings and heterosexuality are used as forms of social control. Instead, the heterosexual imaginary convinces us that what is important is to participate in the legitimizing illusions of the institution. Within some social groupings the arrival of a children is an honored and celebrated event regardless of marital status.

The scale of the celebrity weddings reviewed in *People* and *In Style* is less ostentatious than one might imagine. With a few significant exceptions, most are consistent with national trends, but the wealth and privilege of the families are usually evident in some form of excess, e.g., flowers, other celebrities, cake, special location, or Cinderella coaches. *In Style* places more emphasis on the wedding itself rather than on the celebrity newlyweds. It has a section called "New Tradition: Elements of Style," which highlights the ways music, gowns, and rings say "class act." To accentuate the class standing of celebrities, it lists what kinds of jewelry particular couples give each other. For example, Carolyn Bessette Kennedy (John F. Kennedy, Jr.'s partner) wears an "eternity band of sapphires alternating with white diamonds," and Christie Brinkley's engagement ring is a "hefty sapphire flanked by two diamonds" (*In Style* 1997, 125).

Celebrity is synonymous with spectacle—people wouldn't achieve this status without having already achieved "stardom"—and is the embodiment of spectacle to the consuming public. As a result celebrity weddings alternate between minimalist—getting away from the spotlight—and mega-extravaganza. Either way, media portrayals of celebrity weddings offer a celebration of style, romance, excess, and expense.

Finally, one section of note is *People*'s "Tying the Not" or *In Style*'s "To Be or Knot to Be?" This is where the editors at *People* and *In Style* try to explain why some celebrity couples haven't married or won't marry. "A romantic world wishes they'd wed, but some celebrity couples believe that happily ever after comes without a hitch" (*People* 1997, 168). In other words, marriage in the United States is compulsory. This is not the case worldwide, but the heterosexual imaginary convinces us that marriage is both normal and necessary. Rather than seeing the various interests at stake in decisions of this kind and making fully informed decisions, we instead consent to the illusion that you can't have commitment, love, and family without marriage.

Oprah Winfrey has been "engaged" to Stedman Graham for years and told *Redbook* in 1996 that she has the "right to not get married." Imagine that! She sees this as a right, not a requirement. She also said "I'm sorry I ever was such a bigmouth frog about the engagement." And yet, Oprah is well known for her wedding and bridal gown shows, which give out advice to many viewers seeking to enter

into matrimony. Alan and Denise Fields, the wedding industry consumer advocates, have appeared on her show.

Goldie Hawn and Kurt Russell have been living together for fifteen years. When asked why they hadn't married, Russell commented, "The social prerequisite has no value for me." Hawn, who agrees with Russell, was recently quoted in *Vanity Fair* as saying "I don't believe we own anybody." While numerous other famous couples resist marriage, tabloids and magazines like *People* are invested in the wedding. They know that a wedding featuring any one of these couples would yield higher circulation and greater sales. But beyond this, these periodicals are also invested in the institution and play a significant part in the wedding-ideological complex, securing the future of romance and the social controls necessary for maintaining the status quo. As Katherine Hepburn asserted, "It's bloody impractical to love, honor, and obey. If it weren't, you wouldn't have to sign a contract" (*People* 1997, 168).

"Goin' to the Chapel and We're Gonna Get Married . . ."

The presentation of celebrity weddings by the mass media provides intelligible representations of class for middle-class consumers. Wealth and upper-class status are linked with various forms of conspicuous consumption, which, while excessive, are not unimaginable. For the social elite, the codes of old wealth, while also spectacular, are much more elusive and are frequently concealed behind displays of style and good taste.

The *Sunday New York Times* wedding pages, currently located in the "Sunday Styles" section, are a long-standing institution in American culture. As a site for the wedding announcements of the upper classes, these pages hold particular significance today not just for the upper or owning class but also for the professional-managerial class. With the addition in 1992 of a weekly feature story called "Vows," by Lois Smith Brady, the wedding pages have been updated from their role as part of the "Society" pages, announcing the marriages of young women of the upper class, to include announcements of the weddings of those who are seemingly more typical of *Times* readers.

"To Have and To Hold: From the wealthy about to wed, the prenuptial agreement is the vow that gets honored first. . . .

3. The Precious Bodily Fluid Clauses

Some couples have been using prenuptials to regulate marital behavior. . . . [A] Louisiana man insisted in his prenup that his wife's sexual demands be limited to once a week. He tried to avoid alimony because she violated the prenup by 'seeking coitus thrice daily.' The court ruled in her favor, saying that 'the fault here alleged by the husband is not in law any fault.'"

—Jan Hoffman, *"How They Keep It,"* 1995, p. 104

No longer just about brides and their wedding party, the mainstay of these announcements is the background information revealed about each couple, their families, and their implied social networks. Readers learn not just who is getting married but where they are from and where they were educated. The format for these announcements includes the listing of preparatory schools, if either the bride or groom attended one, which college they each attended, what jobs they each hold, and where they will live. Beyond this, each parent's occupation, volunteer work or other notable endeavor, where they each were educated, and where they reside are included. The listing concludes by mentioning who officiated the ceremony and where the wedding and reception were held.

Inserted subtly into each of these passages is whether or not the bride will take her husband's name. In most cases she complies with patriarchal tradition. In those instances where she has elected to keep her name or hyphenate it with her husband's name, it is often explained as necessary for career continuity.

The context for these announcements is the "Sunday Styles" section, where upper-class interests are cloaked in the guise of style. Each issue contains columns called "Shopping With," featuring famous shoppers and their tastes, "Noticed," about up-and-coming stars or redecorated old celebrities, and "Style Over Substance," explaining current fashion or color preferences, e.g., gray as the "new" black and pink as the "new" orange. Other columns include "A Night Out With," which is an evening version of "Shopping With," and "Pulse," which offers color photos and small text boxes of emerging trends in fashion and leisure activities. "On the Street" provides a collage of photos illustrating the everyday use of high style and good use of fashion trends, presumably apparent just by walking around Manhattan. And, finally, on the page preceding the wedding announcements is the former high-society page now called "Evening Hours." This is comprised of a black-and-white-photo collage of the rich and famous gathering for either celebrity, arts, or charity events. These photos give *Times* readers a window into the upper-class social world by revealing who they are, what causes they support, and what their social networks are. Interestingly, however, celebrity weddings are not spotlighted in this section. The reader learns what counts as upper-class style without the spectacle of the photo spread used by magazines such as *People* and *In Style*.

"Think of her as Robobride, equal parts Martha Stewart and Arnold Schwarznegger. In increasing numbers, women in the 20's and 30's are seeking professional help to sculpture a body that's fit to walk the aisle. . . . The trend is driven in large part by the evolution in wedding dress styles—from the overblown Cinderella look chosen by the Princess of Wales . . . to the satin slip worn by Carolyn Bessette-Kennedy. . . . 'I realized all eyes were going to be on me. He's in a tuxedo . . . but there's 200 of them out there, and this is the memory they're going to keep of you, frozen in time.'"

—Stephen Henderson, "Get Me to the Gym on Time," 1998, p. 9.1

Lead articles in "Sunday Styles" include large color photos and provide maga-zine-like, glitzy coverage of contemporary trends for the rich and famous. For example, some of the recent topics have included "How the Glitz Stole Greenwich" (subtitled "In a town where wealth used to whisper, new residents are turning up the volume") or "This Year, the Jet Set is Seeking Nirvana" (subtitled "In an age of cell-phone gurus and E-mail ashrams, trend setters go East to scratch a spiritual itch and play 'Zennis'"). In fact, the only discussion of weddings short of the wed-ding announcements and "Vows" is an occasional article on upscale wedding trends such as the recent "Get Me to the Gym on Time" (subtitled "Brides are mak-ing sure that what they show is shapely").

"Vows," by Lois Smith Brady, is a regular column in the Sunday wedding pages. It features a large and small photo of some moment in a selected newlywed's cou-pled life or wedding. What's significant about these photos is the elusiveness of their subjects. They provide a glimpse into a wedding or the couple's lives togeth-er but from what seems, at first, to be an unusual photo location—e.g., the back of the church, over some spectator's shoulder, the receiving line, the center of clink-ing glasses, in their kitchen. The photographer never allows the viewer the oppor-tunity to witness or consume the central wedding image. Instead, by their subjects' elusiveness and the context, these photos seem to preserve the privacy of the fea-tured couple while conveying both style and chic, concealing from view the class interests operating here.

Consistent with the spectacle of accumulation, the narrative that accompanies the photos is primarily about the romance between the bride and the groom. It gives some of the same information provided in the other wedding announce-ments but fills in with a story about the couple—their childhoods, their dreams and interests, and any significant obstacle they may have overcome to get to this point. Commonplace in this column are stories about couples facing life-threat-ening diseases or disabling accidents or momentary lapses in employment in the arts. Central to these stories, however, is how the bride and groom met and how romantic their relationship has been, including, in some cases, a story about the engagement proposal. These accounts usually conclude with a summary of the cer-emony, including the location, the music played, and something interesting about the reception, including an occasional quote from a loving parent.

Still, while the "Vows" quarter-page column appears to reveal a story about the experience and romance of wedding, it has the strange effect of leaving the reader with far less than if they had read about the couple in *People* or *In Style*. The difference, of course, is that these are generally not celebrity weddings—though on occasion, a celebrity guest credentials the couple with their presence at the wedding. Additionally, these articles convey an "everyday" kind of quality about the subjects while, at the same, preserving the class interests of the publication itself and the audience it addresses and serves.

What is significant about the wedding announcements is the inclusion of the bride's and groom's education and career. This is a recent trend in *New York Times* wedding announcements, reflecting the historical necessity of work in the lives of the upper classes. Most of the couples represented here are from the professional-managerial class, where all difference is homogenized into a collage of well-educated, career-oriented couples. Each listing begins with their education and occupations, a very different focus over other popular culture representations. What separates this class from the others is the primacy of occupation and career over romance and the rise of women into professional or leadership careers. The only differences evident in the listings are those of race and ethnicity. The vast majority of couples included in these pages are white, with a few obvious—only because of their rarity—exceptions. Between August 1997 and August 1998, for example, only 9.5 percent of the couples whose photographs appeared in these pages qualified as people of color or nonwhite.

While the wedding-page photographs of couples are more commonplace today, these pages still frequently feature pictures of brides, and wedding announcements still begin with the bride's background. This pattern, while breaking to some degree from earlier periods where only the bride was featured, reinforces the notion that the wedding is primarily of interest to women.

Typically, wedding announcements in the *New York Times* represent two groups: couples who are finished with college (some either in or finished with graduate school) and older couples remarrying and settled in their careers. In one example from January 1998, a white heterosexual couple in their forties is photographed in professional attire, their heads together, and smiling into the camera. Below their photo, the announcement focuses on their credentials and social networks. Most of this announcement is devoted to telling the bride's history, occupation, credentials, and family connections. While she might appear nontraditional to the middle-class reader, this narrative fits the norm for her social class.

The social networks in evidence in this announcement are substantial. Links to the federal government, the executive branch, the Senate, the Judiciary and the Department of Justice, and the Department of State all appear. The couple, one a high-level lawyer and the other a medical specialist, will also have access to the legal profession and to the medical establishment as well as to two different universities. Their ages and that they were each previously married indicate that they've had much longer than traditional-age couples to accumulate resources and property. The bride's mother also has connections to the arts. Because of all of these factors the access and privilege afforded this couple by virtue of their class is extensive and powerful. This announcement signals to all of the participants in these networks that this couple's social capital will increase and be available to other members of the same circles.

The second group represented in these announcements is comprised of people in their mid- to late twenties or early thirties who are marrying for the first time. In one typical example from August 1998, both the bride and the groom are aspiring professionals who have attended prestigious or Ivy League colleges and universities and have completed graduate work in topics and disciplines—art history and classical studies—which are out of the mainstream and not very marketable for the average college graduate. Given their class access, this lack of marketability is not apparent. From the description in the announcement, which leads off with the bride's accomplishments, they have already established connections in the professional-managerial class that will allow them to advance and diversify. With an air of confidence and a sense of direction, the couple reveal their plans to work together in related jobs while the groom completes his doctoral research in classical studies. The bride has chosen to take her husband's name and, though she is credentialed and has a job opportunity in her field, will work in an overseas location compatible with her groom's professional development.

Related to these "credential capsules" are the "Vows" columns, which also appear in each Sunday edition. While the announcements authorize the couple in their own social networks, the narratives in "Vows" provide an ideological tool for the upper classes. Generally, the professional-managerial class bride and groom in these stories is presented as the "everyday" or "just folk" couple. In keeping with the "Style" theme of this section, newlyweds are frequently portrayed as progressive, well connected, tasteful, "hip," and occasionally multiethnic.

Ideologically, "Vows" works to certify the professional-managerial class as "average" and makes romance and the wedding seem natural, ordinary, and glamorous. The heterosexual imaginary is particularly visible in these stories. Erased from view are the interests of the dominant social order that "needs" to recruit middle-class women into new jobs while preserving patriarchal social arrangements. Rosemary Hennessy, in her book *Materialist Feminism and the Politics of Discourse*, refers to this process as the production of the "New Woman":

> Capitalism in the post-industrial west, increasingly in competition with the "third world," has had to revise, readjust, and even abandon altogether the ideology of separate spheres in order to draw more middle-class women into its labor force. Doing that without risking the patriarchal symbolic order has required delicate renegotiations of the . . . feminine. Throughout the twentieth century these renegotiations have taken the form of various versions of the New Woman. Most recently she is figured as the professional career woman, often juggling work with domestic responsibilities of "home and family." (1993a, 106)

To do this, the heterosexual imaginary circulating in the "Vows" columns attempts to construct appealing images of this "new woman" who is able to accommodate and give priority to domestic life while managing her professional responsibilities as well. The stories presented in these columns mask the contradictions underlying weddings, marriage, and heterosexuality by romanticizing certain images and suppressing others that threaten the legitimacy of these arrangements. Julie Torrant, in her unpublished article "For Better or Worse: Marriage in Commodity Culture," explains how this process depends upon the ideological work of sites such as the "Styles" section of the *Times* and the column "Vows" through the "transference of the old order onto new ideas, signs, and activities" (1998, 15).

One of the ideological strategies "Vows" uses to achieve this process is romance. To manage social differences within the couple, a typical pattern in these narratives is to provide an explanation for the potential mismatch of two very different people. The story then resolves this situation by demonstrating how romance and love conquer all. Removing the names of the newlyweds from the actual narratives, the following section provides an in-depth examination of these processes.

In the spring of 1998, "Vows" feature writer Lois Smith Brady covered the wedding of Clara Binder and Lenny Solar (the names in this story have been changed). The lead photo for this article shows just the hands of wedding guests toasting with champagne glasses. The smaller photo insert shows the bride and groom in wedding regalia looking at themselves in a mirror experiencing the joy of the heterosexual imaginary, examining their own wedding reflection.

The article begins "they were as different as yoga and high-impact aerobics." He is the owner of a home furnishings store in an upscale New York neighborhood and brings with him the knowledge and sensibility associated with "making your home a sanctuary, an ecologically aware oasis full of fresh flowers, favorite scents and couches you can sink into like mud baths." Her apartment is "about as comforting to the soul as junk mail," and Brady characterizes her as a "super-serious career woman" who is employed as a buyer for a clothing catalog and has little time for domestic responsibilities.

Within the first couple of paragraphs we become aware that they have different priorities, different tastes, different values, and may come from different classes. We also observe some reversal of traditional heterogendered behaviors: he's more concerned with the domestic sphere and she is career-driven. But as a column anchoring the wedding pages of a major newspaper, "Vows" must have a happy ending; the reader is invited, therefore, to imagine how this little drama will reach its inevitable conclusion.

When they first meet, they experience an instant attraction, but Lenny is already married and they opt to become close friends. Meanwhile, Clara recognizes she is "falling in love" and distances herself from Lenny. She finds a boyfriend, and Lenny stays with his wife. At this point in the tale, the dominant ideology concerning monogamous marriage is still intact, and "Vows" does its part to reassure us.

A year later, Lenny calls Clara and says he is getting a divorce and would like to have dinner. Clara leaps at the chance by saying, "Great, let's go." They go out to dinner, kiss goodnight, and Clara returns home and tells her boyfriend to move out. As this story unfolds in the telling of a "happily-ever-after" wedding tale, the heterosexual imaginary works to suppress the reasons for "falling in love" as well as the breaking-up-with-boyfriend story. In the interests of "the wedding," "falling in love" is taken for granted, and monogamous heterosexuality without marriage is subordinated to the wedding story. A committed and live-in relationship without the wedding ring and the sanction of state and religion doesn't count. The need for the *vow* is secured.

Predictably, Clara's life becomes transformed by Lenny's interest in home furnishings and poetry. "He introduced me to a whole other world I never knew existed," she said. Another difference Brady points out about these two people is their ages—Lenny is 45 and Clara is 31. As the narrative continues, we see Clara become more and more domesticated and mature, leveling not just their gender and class differences but their age differences as well. In the midst of all the style and good taste (read class) Lenny brings to her life, Clara must hide one of her trademarks, a "large jar of dingy pennies"—she no longer thinks it looks very good. She is assimilating into her new class position.

After learning she was pregnant, Clara and Lenny became engaged. Brady assesses the situation: "With a baby due in August, she says she is feeling more domestic and has transformed from a woman obsessed with her resumé to one fascinated with recipes." The transformation is nearly complete. This new woman, this 90s professional-managerial woman, is about become an upper-middle-class mother and wife.

The ideology of romantic love permeates the description of the ceremony, and, as Torrant explains, "works to naturalize the hierarchy of romantic relationships over work relationships between men and women, and thus also works to naturalize heterosexuality" (1998, 17). The storybook wedding concludes with "a down-

pour of rose petals thrown by friends," the groom crying and trying to avoid stain-
ing his very stylish "platinum Commes de Garçons suit," and the "completely
thrilled" bride adorned in a Mary Adams couture gown of "sleeveless silk taffeta,"
"a wrinkly skirt, a tiered organza overskirt and a furry boa."

In preserving the interests of the wedding industry, Lois Smith Brady ends her
piece on Clara and Lenny with quotes from the gown designer and the jewelry
designer. The former asserts, "She [the bride] was completely thrilled that everything was happening at once." The latter claims, "There's a tremendous romance
in being pregnant and getting married. . . . You have a baby, you have marriage,
and you have love." Since the author and the two speakers at the end are all female,
the alliance of women to carry out the mission of the dominant social order works
to secure the consent of women to these arrangements. In the end, the interests
of patriarchal heterosexuality and capitalism are both preserved. Clara is both wife
and worker without endangering the order of either sphere.

Through the telling of these wedding stories, "Vows" teaches us what counts as
a "vow." It is making a commitment to preserve the dominant social order. The
vow is the securing of consent to the terms of the dominant class.

The power of the heterosexual imaginary circulating in these stories and in popular culture cannot be overstated. We begin by naturalizing gender as though it is
somehow related to our biology and not the result of social processes or organized
in the interests of institutionalized heterosexuality. Obscured from view are the
powerful ruling interests being served by this institution. Weddings, marriage,
romance, and heterosexuality become naturalized to the point where we consent
to the belief that marriage is necessary to achieve a sense of well-being, belonging,
passion, morality, and love. And we live with the illusion that marriage is somehow linked to the natural order of the universe rather than see it as it is: a social
and cultural practice produced to serve particular interests.

These same beliefs also prevent us from imagining childbearing and childrea-
ring as legitimate without state-regulated marriage. Instead we conduct studies of
children of divorce and examine the "problems" of "broken homes" and of the loss
of "family values" without ever calling into question the very structures that create
the conditions that produce these outcomes. By allowing the heterosexual imagi-

nary to circulate freely with our consent and without question, we participate in the production and perpetuation of racial, class, gender, and sexual hierarchies; legitimize ruling interests; and fail to provide our children with the imaginations and skills they need to become critical citizens of the world. The institution of heterosexuality as it is currently organized serves the interests of capitalist patriarchy, functions as a form of social control, and depends upon the heterosexual imaginary to conceal its regulatory function and effects. Ultimately we've allowed for the romancing of the clone.

"This morning . . . the Walt Disney Corporation announced a partnership with Pfizer Corporation in the marketing of the breakthrough sex drug Viagra. . . . Disney's theme parks are among the most popular destinations for newlyweds. A marketing partnership promoting the new drug could do the same thing for those people traveling on second honeymoons."

DND Wirenews (20 May 98) — Lake Buena Vista, Fl.

Chapter Four

Four Weddings and an Industry

Popular Film and Television Weddings

In the quote above, Howard Brackett's mother has just learned, by way of an Oscar acceptance speech from her son's former student, Cameron Drake, that Howard may be gay. With Howard's wedding just three days away, this revelation comes as a shock to Mr. and Mrs. Brackett, who make it very clear to their son that even if he is gay, he *will* get married whether he wants to or not. At one point, Mrs. Brackett asks, "I can understand that he's gay, but why wouldn't he want a wedding?" Of course, this line is intended to be humorous, but the humor depends upon certain assumptions about the audience. The filmmakers expect the viewer to think this is absurd, laughable. Why would anyone think it's understandable to be gay? At the same time, they expect the audience to find it unimaginable that anyone wouldn't want a wedding. The combination of these two assumptions works to naturalize both institutionalized heterosexuality and its organizing rituals, exemplifying one of the dominant themes in wedding-oriented movies and television shows.

The foundational assumptions in this quote illustrate how some of these ideologies circulate. First, by the string of associations she lays out, Howard's mother asserts her "unconditional" love for her son, indicating that she will love him regardless of how bad or awful he might be. Using the dominant way of thinking about difference, she associates "gay" with color, crime, violence, and murder and places "gay" in a string of descriptors that signify criminal, ugly, unnatural, and deviant. The race theme also surfaces here in her reference to color. While it is somewhat subverted by mentioning red/green as opposed to black/white, the invocation of the color code has the same consequence. According to this passage, to be "of color" is to be "out of the ordinary."

Second, she asserts the primacy of the wedding with her emphasis on the "need" to marry. In her mind, weddings and marriage are natural and compulsory, not optional and certainly not something to take lightly.

Third, she tells us what a wedding means. It is about beauty and order and the desire to escape the real world. The message about heroin is very important here. It is the defining signifier of this passage, making it clear that the wedding is much more than a ritual. It is addictive, compulsory, a "have-to-have." It is the heterosexual imaginary at work, the moment for creating the illusion of happiness, order, well-being, and plenitude. It is the event that allows us to feel comfortable with the dominant social order, conceal any of its contradictions, and anesthetize ourselves against an everyday "state of affairs which needs illusions."[1] Weddings are ritual, drugged, and "feel-good" experiences. Mom needs a fix!

This chapter assesses two cultural sites—wedding movies and television shows—for evidence of the power relations organizing both allowed and disallowed meanings. Each of the examples studied makes use of the traditional white wedding theme with a white bride in a white wedding gown. Also, in each instance the cast is white. The films selected for this study include *The Birdcage, Father of the Bride II, Four Weddings and a Funeral, In & Out, My Best Friend's Wedding,* and *The Wedding Singer.* These will be considered in relation to a selection of prime-time television weddings from shows during the same decade: *Ally McBeal, Cheers, Coach, Drew Carey, Ellen, Friends, Heart's Afire, Jag, L.A. Law, Lois & Clark, Mad About You, The Nanny, Northern Exposure, Everybody Loves Raymond, Roseanne, Suddenly Susan, Third Rock from the Sun, Who's the Boss,* and *90210.*

"And We'll Never Be Lonely Any More . . ."

"'Party of Five' star Jennifer Love Hewitt's next project is a real dream. It's called 'Cupid's Love,' a romantic comedy about a wedding planner who falls for the groom. The story came to her in her sleep. 'I had a dream about it, and I woke up and wrote a treatment for it. Then I went to see some producer friends of mine and sort of jokingly pitched them this idea.' . . . Hewitt reportedly got six figures for the pitch alone."

—Albany Times Union, "Dream Comes True for Actress's Movie Concept," October 11, 1998, A2

The visual media constitutes the most affective site in the wedding-industrial and -ideological complexes. By providing compelling images, popular film and television commodify weddings and create the market, the desire, and the demand for the white wedding. Watching our favorite actors achieve happiness or love allows us to live vicariously through the experiences of characters with whom we identify and grow to love and appreciate. The visual simulation of the wedding story is a powerful means for suturing an audience to the interests represented in a film or television show. Even though most of us are able to separate fantasy from reality, we still experience these stories and the emotions they evoke on the level of both the conscious and the unconscious. It's possible to be both critically aware of this medium while simultaneously crying or laughing with the characters. The romantic illusions created by media weddings construct desire to such an extent that, without realizing it, we place these illusions above reality. When the average bride spending $823 on a wedding gown, $19,000 on a wedding, and incurring a wedding debt far beyond her means, it appears the wedding-ideological complex is succeeding.

Messages from these films make their way into the cultural real—the culturally constructed world as opposed to the real world—in very powerful ways. Consider, for example, the now legendary attack on single motherhood by former Vice President Dan Quayle, who assailed the fictional character Murphy Brown for her irresponsibility in having a child out of wedlock. Touchstone Pictures' *Father of the Bride* and *Father of the Bride II* was so successful in capturing the imaginations of the American public that Disney, the parent company for Touchstone, developed their own Fairy Tale Wedding Pavilion complete with wedding consultants and spaces modeled on the film. In a recent commercial advertising the upcoming wedding of *The Nanny*, cast members talked about what a beautiful wedding it was, as though an actual wedding had occurred. These instances are indicative of the influential role popular film and television have on how we think about ourselves, other people, and our values and on how we should behave in the real world. But more

than that, they support a wedding-industrial complex that needs the romance fantasy in order to keep weddings and marriage desirable and profitable. Using the heterosexual imaginary, the visual media are highly effective in communicating how to imagine weddings, romance, marriage, and heterosexuality. Consent to the wedding industry, the dominant class, and the capitalist patriarchal social order is assured by the popularity of these images.

Films and television are well liked in part because the tales they present are intelligible to us. The comprehensibility they produce is a product of dominant ideologies about marriage combined with utopian notions of love and community, a dash of male resistance, and a hint of alternatives, circulating in the culture-at-large as well as in the guise of entertainment and escape. These media tales make use of the romance-novel, fairy-tale formula made familiar to many—especially women—since early childhood.

One of the ways these meaning-making processes work is by providing the viewer with stories and visuals that represent our class position, bind us to it, and manage the contradictions we see in the world around us. For example, Oprah Winfrey can provide numerous shows on affordable weddings, wedding gowns, and even wedding consumer advocacy, yet she can claim her "right" not to marry, violating the heterosexual prescription for acceptability—that all eligible women must marry. This contradiction is managed by her service to the middle class through her public celebration of weddings and marriage as well as by her class standing. People can make sense of her as a legitimate exception because of dominant beliefs about fame and wealth that justify her perceived desire to protect her power.

One of the central objectives of the mass media is to provide the images necessary to reproduce the ruling order. As Douglas Kellner points out in his essay "Cultural Studies, Multiculturalism and Media Culture,"

> Media images help shape our view of the world and our deepest values:
> what we consider good or bad, positive or negative, moral or evil. Media
> stories provide the symbols, myths and resources through which we
> constitute a common culture. . . . Media spectacles demonstrate who

From Harper's, an actual letter from a bride to her wedding party:

*"Dear Bridal Party,
. . . I've never wanted a small country-type wedding—Z says this is no wedding but rather a coronation!! Well, not quite. But it sure has been fun so far, and I just cannot wait for everyone to arrive and for all our friends and relatives to have one great, fabulous night. . . . Won't each of you come with Z and me to fantasy land—a place where dreams come true and fun abounds for everyone? Where the bride is Cinderella and the groom is the Prince for an evening. You are going to attend a ball at 'Buckingham Palace' (pretend) and the King and Queen have invited only 'royalty'—YOU! This will be a time to remember when you were courting the person to whom you are now married. . . . If you have a happy marriage now . . . we expect the Palace to be really electrified with all that LOVE. May your every dream come true! Love, X"*

> has the power and who is powerless. . . . They dramatize and legitimate
> the power of the forces that be and show the powerless that they must
> stay in their places or be destroyed. . . . Ideologies make inequalities and
> subordination appear natural and just and thus induce consent to
> relations of domination. (1995, 5)

Consistent with Kellner's argument, weddings in popular culture are powerful sites for the enactment of dominant messages about society-at-large. Film and television industries know just how to use weddings to reflect and reproduce the kinds of messages necessary to ensure compliance with the dominant social order as they secure their own interests and markets.

In the presentation of wedding stories in popular film and television, the heterosexual imaginary makes the social order appear more manageable and comfortable. Using the power celebrities hold as the embodiment of fantasy to authorize particular social behaviors and beliefs, the visual media demonstrate where the margin of acceptability begins and ends. By making visible the consequences of operating outside the norm or the constructed "natural," the film industry legitimizes ruling interests and gains our compliance with practices that keep power in place. For example, the consumption of tales of romance, while profit-making for the producers of soap operas, romance novels, romantic comedies, and media weddings, prevents us from seeing the underlying material consequences (see Chapter 2) these images and practices allow. They promote the "structured invisibility" of whiteness, numb us to excess, and police the boundaries of social acceptability around categories of race, class, sexuality, and even beauty.

In concert with some of the other components of the wedding-ideological complex examined in the previous chapter, weddings in popular film and television contribute to the *creation of many taken-for-granted beliefs, values, and assumptions about weddings.* This wedding-ideological complex works to naturalize romance, weddings, marriage, and heterosexuality rather than present them as the result of meaning-making systems that organize what may or may not be the "natural" world. For example, in *all* of the film and television weddings studied in this chapter, the following references were made by or about the bride:

"It's my wedding day!"

"I've been planning for this day all my life (or since I was . . .)"

"I want a storybook wedding."

"It's the most important day of my life."

"I've waited my whole life for this day."

"Everything has to be (is) perfect."

"This will be the perfect wedding with the perfect guy."

"This is the happiest day of my life."

"I have to have the perfect wedding dress."

The pervasiveness of these messages is a sign of the intense socialization effort that the wedding-ideological complex has undertaken in constructing femininity, heterosexuality, and the importance of weddings to a woman's identity. What does it mean that the most important day of a woman's life is her wedding day? Why go on living after it's over? These messages are so powerful that even when characters in films and television weddings—not to mention women in real life—acknowledge the artificiality of these messages, it is still in the context of "Oh, well, I still want a wedding" or "I guess I'm just old-fashioned." Recently, a friend of mine confessed, "I tried on my old wedding dress, and, I hate to tell you this, but it felt great!" While many women comply with dominant messages about femininity, heterosexuality, and weddings, some participate in the white wedding mill for other reasons. Weddings can represent a form of resistance among women who must face the social pressures of the workplace and other responsibilities. They can claim the romantic illusion of guarantees, kept promises, and well-being created by the wedding as a way to escape the strain of their real conditions of existence. Regardless of the motivation, the naturalization of the white wedding has been enormously successful.

Cultural theorist Mas'ud Zavarzadeh, in his book *Seeing Films Politically*, argues that this naturalization process is necessary to the reproduction of ruling interests. In using the example of the social production of femininity, Zavarzadeh's argument pertains to the institution it organizes—heterosexuality:

> Capitalist patriarchy . . . requires an idea of femininity that reproduces its relations of production and thus perpetuates itself without any serious challenge to its fundamental social norms. . . . None of these [feminine] traits are in themselves and "by nature" definitive of femininity and all are in fact political attributes required for maintaining asymmetrical power relations and thus the exploitative gender relations between men and women. . . . These traits, however, are not produced in a material vacuum: a society "desires" that which is historically necessary for its reproduction and can be made intelligible to its members. (1991, 93)

The examination of white weddings in popular film and television provides some clues concerning the interests society "needs" to serve in this historical moment. Identifying the ideological strategies used in films allows us to unpack the beliefs created about social relations and gives us a critical stance from which to examine our participation in naturalizing them.

"What's Love Got to Do with It?"

With the ratings success of soap opera weddings, these melodramtic ceremonies have also become main fare for prime-time television, capturing the much-coveted consumer market of "18- to 49-year-old women" (Lipton 1992, 1). May "sweeps week," when television networks compete for the largest share of the viewing audience, has become synonymous with wedding shows. Stations usually save their most spectacular production for that week in hopes of eliminating the competition. In an article in *Detroit News* in May 1996, Michael McWilliams reported that "Weddings are the Icing for the May Sweeps":

> You know it's the May sweeps when everybody on TV gets married. Tonight's Must See TV, for example, turns into Must Say I Do, when three NBC sitcoms—**Friends, Seinfeld,** and **Caroline in the City**—crack wise at the altar, or very near it. . . . Amid all these wedding bells, marriages

figure prominently this month in shows as disparate as **Ellen,** and
Melrose Place, The John Larroquette Show and **Homicide: Life on the
Street,** not exactly known for its romantic bliss. (1996, 7)

The trend that McWilliams identifies has continued into the late 1990s and shows
no signs of abating. The 1997–98 season opened with weddings, e.g., *Dharma and
Greg*, and closed with them on *Friends, The Nanny, Jag, Spin City, Baywatch, Suddenly Susan, Dr. Quinn, Everybody Loves Raymond, NYPD Blue*, and *For Your Love*.
This year, the 1998–99 season began with the conclusion of the *Friends* wedding
that closed the previous season, carrying the wedding theme through a total of four
episodes. *To Have & To Hold* and *Will & Grace* each began their new seasons with
weddings. Made-for-tv movies that will include weddings during the same time
period include *Forever Love, The Marriage Fool, A Marriage of Convenience*, and *I
Married a Monster*. (See Appendix for listing of wedding movies.)

A similar trend can be seen in the film industry. While the mainstream formula for success used to be "tits and ass" with a dash of violence, contemporary
motion pictures include weddings regardless of their relevance to the film. Besides
the box office success of *Father of the Bride* and *Father of the Bride* II (1991), subsequent films such as *Four Weddings and a Funeral, My Best Friend's Wedding, The
Wedding Singer, In & Out, Muriel's Wedding, The Wedding Banquet*, and *The Polish
Wedding* have opened the space for the continuing production of wedding films
because of their box office success. Even action films such as *Armaggedon*, which
typically draw a predominantly young male audience, now include a big white
wedding.

The increased prevalence of weddings in popular film and television in the
1990s provides an important opportunity to examine and make visible what the
culture "permits" us to believe about romance, weddings, marriage, and heterosexuality. Particular patterns coalesce in the telling of film or television wedding
stories to produce a taken-for-granted social order that naturalizes practices that
are anything but natural. The creation of social givens, such as weddings and heterosexuality, requires the use of a variety of meaning-making strategies that invite
both affirmation and participation in the practices of the dominant class. In the

popular films and television shows covered in this chapter, four ideological themes dominate: 1) romantic love and heterogender; 2) marriage and heterosexual supremacy; 3) social difference; and 4) class and accumulation. These meaning-making systems appear in varying combinations in each of the films and television shows examined in this study.

"Here Comes the Bride, All Dressed in White. . . ."

The ideology of romantic love and the ideology of heterogender intersect in depictions of weddings in popular culture. Romance, most often expressed as the illusion of well-being, is central to the selling of media weddings. Romance represents the utopian promise of love, joy, happiness, well-being, belonging, and community. Ultimately, romance is ideology at work in the creation of illusion. It is not about the real but is, instead, about the fantasy, fairy-tale, or utopian vision of the real. Applied to weddings and the institution of heterosexuality, romance works in the service of the heterosexual imaginary. Embedded within the film romance are messages about the value of weddings and marriage. In the heterogendered division of labor, romance is primarily the domain of women, or the emotive side of labor. It is the work of women within heterogendered social arrangements to do the work of feeling and caring as well as the work of providing an affective environment and of eliciting emotion from her partner. It is central to the invisible labor of women whether it be at home or in the workplace, e.g., mother, wife, flight attendant, nurse, therapist (DeVault 1991; Hochschild 1985; Smith 1987). As Marj DeVault explains in her 1991 study *Feeding the Family: The Social Organization of Caring as Gendered Work:*

> Though necessary for maintaining the social world as we have known it, caring has been mostly unpaid work, traditionally undertaken by women, activity whose value is not fully acknowledged even by those who do it. . . . Social expectation has made the undefined, unacknowledged activity central to women's identity. . . . Both men and women have learned to think of these patterns as "natural." (3)

Popular culture plays a key role in naturalizing these patterns, and weddings are sites for the standardization of this heterogendered division of labor. Women's labor is usually both invisible and considered a personal service outside of capital; the bride exemplifies this. The spectacle precedes isolation and the experience of putting men first.

In four of the movies and in virtually all of the television weddings covered in this book, romance plays a pivotal role in setting up the subordinate position of women in relation to men. Over and over again we get the message that romance and wedding planning is the separate sphere of women or women's work. *Father of the Bride* revolves around the commiseration of Dad, who complains, scowls, and is mystified by how his wife and daughter spend "his" money in the name of a beautiful romantic white wedding. The image created in this movie is of two women sparing no expense to make sure this is the "wedding of a lifetime," one that is befitting the great love the bride-to-be Annie Banks (Kimberly Williams) has found with the groom-to-be Bryan MacKenzie (George Newbern).

The success of this film depends upon the intersection of several ideological frames: prevailing beliefs about romance and the heterogendered division of labor, and their link to class and accumulation interests. For example, in the opening scene of the movie we are greeted by George Banks (Steve Martin), the father of the bride, owner of a successful shoe factory, immediately after the wedding of his daughter Annie Banks-MacKenzie. The father of the bride confides to the audience: "I'll tell you a secret. This wedding cost more than this house when we bought it seventeen years ago. I'm told I'll look back on this day with affection and nostalgia. I hope so." This whole scene lasts for several minutes, as Banks recounts for the audience—and particularly fathers—what they should expect to encounter when their daughters marry. With a mixture of nostalgia for the little girl who once sat on his lap and called him "her hero" combined with complaints about expenses, this opening monologue teaches the audience that weddings are the irrational and expensive domain of women—the irrational and spendthrift sex.

The film makes use of the heterogender stereotype of women as consumers and as hopeless romantics spending excessively to provide something men find both painful and unintelligible unless, of course, they happen to be Franck Eggelhoffer

"On Friday, January 17, 1992, Angela, her fiancé, Michael, and three other couples were married in the lobby of an AMC Theater in Hollywood, Florida. The ceremony, which Rick and Suds broadcast live, featured theater ushers acting as, well, ushers and a notary who addressed the brides as Cinderella and the grooms as Prince Charming. It was held to promote Touchstone Pictures' Father of the Bride, a gentle comedy that has about as much to do with reality as Disneyland does—particularly in its depiction of family values, family life, and family finances. But that's why we go to the movies."

—John Clark, "Bride and Joy," p. 108

(Martin Short), the effeminate wedding coordinator. The ideological work of this film is to delineate the heterogendered division of labor portraying Dad as successful factory owner and Mom and daughter as women who spend his money frivolously. What is interesting about this film is how it both trivializes and elevates women's interest in weddings in an effort to secure both a female and male audience and preserve patriarchal heterosexuality and the heterogendered division of labor.

With refrains of "A wedding's a big deal!" and "We have to have a wedding coordinator" and "Welcome to the '90s, George!" from Nina Banks (Diane Keaton), the mother of the bride and George's wife, combined with the father's romance with his daughter, an estimated expenditure of about $45,000 is legitimized, twice the cost of the average American wedding. To convey to the viewer a "Father Knows Best" middle-America backdrop to this wedding, the filmmakers use two devices. First, they provide small-town, Main Street images of Dad coming home from work as he narrates how he's not "big on change," "loves this small town," and enjoys every facet of parenting. The first time we see Dad with his daughter is when she returns from a semester in Italy. He hurries home to see her, telling us how much he loves his big white colonial house with the white picket fence and how the best part of this house is the family life it's made possible. He's greeted at the door by his wife and young son and is warned that his daughter, Annie, has changed. Annie greets him by sliding down the banister into his arms, calling up images of what she's probably done since she was a small child, and reassuring him that she hasn't changed that much.

Ideological notions of middle-class, middle-American, traditional family values are securely established in the first ten minutes of this film. This depiction of the white middle-class marriage and family makes use of a number of images already firmly in place in the collective imagination. By calling up themes from *Father Knows Best, Leave it to Beaver,* or *The Donna Reed Show, Father of the Bride* naturalizes notions of the traditional, nuclear, middle-class family and removes from view the reality that such media constructions are historical and serve particular socioeconomic interests.

Later in the movie, we have the opportunity to see "real," big-city wealth when the Banks are invited to visit with the groom's family, the MacKenzies of Los Angeles. They live in a gated community in Bel Air and own "the biggest house on the street." While they present themselves as everyday, nice people, their wealth and privilege is made visible in a variety of ways. As George moves through their house, his thoughts are revealed to the viewer: "All I could think about was the size of this place. I could have parked our whole house in the foyer." When George asks where the bathroom is, Mrs. MacKenzie directs him to the "seventh door on the left" on the second floor, signaling to the audience the enormity of this house and the MacKenzies' wealth. The contrasts between upper-class and middle-class trappings work to suture the viewer to the class "plight" of the Banks. Even though Mr. and Mrs. Banks are both business owners, the audience is invited to sympathize with their "lack," or relative poverty. The film attempts to conceal the class privilege of the Banks by accentuating the excesses of MacKenzies.

As the story progresses and we watch George's frustration with the excesses of the wedding preparations and the wealthiness of the MacKenzies, the film works to comfort the white middle-class viewer with complaints about consumer rip-offs and feelings of economic inadequacy. The story line of this film depends upon the viewing audience identifying with the Bankses and appreciating the contrasts and discomforts between small town and big city, middle-class income and upper-class wealth. Significant in these contrasts is the way they also legitimize the $45,000 wedding for the middle class as well as the interests of the owning class. The expense of this wedding is justified as an expression of the love of the parents for their daughter and as "affordable" for the middle-class family, which may have to give up some things but puts the interests of their child's "special day" ahead of any practicality or notion of excess.

Four Weddings and a Funeral, My Best Friend's Wedding, and television weddings on *Suddenly Susan* and *The Nanny* make use of similar ideological devices in that they all provide examples of extraordinarily expensive weddings as reasonable and natural, supporting the interests of the wedding-industrial complex. In each of these examples the weddings represented easily equal or exceed the $45,000 model in *Father of the Bride.* Justifications for these expenditures are virtually invisible and become normalized through the invocation of the "special" romance that

"She was working in a bridal shop in Flushing, Queens, 'til her boyfriend kicked her out in one of those crushing scenes . . ."

Verse from the theme song for the television show The Nanny

requires such class trappings. Of course, all of the examples mentioned thus far are of the traditional white wedding with the white bride in a white wedding gown. *Four Weddings* even goes so far as to provide the viewer with four weddings of varying elegance and opulence, reinforcing the normalization of the upper-class white wedding spectacle.

Beyond the development of the white wedding as a standardizing practice for late-twentieth-century capitalism, these images also convey the illusion that the institution of heterosexuality is stable, made up of promises and dreams fulfilled, and invulnerable to crisis or disruption. Considering the various social forces pressuring marriage in the late 1990s, these images are both the product of resistance to the realities of contemporary heterosexuality and the construction of propertied interests that depend upon these notions for their survival.

Combined with markers of class and wealth, nearly *all* of the films and television shows considered in this book carry the traditionally heterogendered ideological message about patriarchal heterosexuality. While each of these stories provides an example of the "new woman" of the 1990s—someone who has a career, owns her own business, or has access to the professional-managerial class—subordination to the interests of the husband is romantic, feminine, and normal. In Annie's exchange with her father in *Father of the Bride* when she announces to her family that she is engaged to be married, she argues that she can be both wife and her "own person."

> Dad: I thought you didn't believe in marriage. I thought it meant a woman lost her identity. I thought you wanted to get a job before you settled down and earn money and be your own person.

> Annie: All right. I didn't think I believed in marriage until I met Bryan. Bryan's not like any other man I've ever known. I **want** to be married to him. I'm not going to lose my identity with him. He's not some overpowering macho guy. . . . He's like you, Dad! Except he's brilliant. (sigh) I'm not going to marry some ape who'll want me to wear go-go boots and an apron.

Reminiscent of stories in the *New York Times* "Vows" column, Annie will pursue her career but will give priority to her marriage *and* to her new husband. The values she espoused about not complying with marriage disappear in the blush of romance. As Annie goes through this explanation with her father, her mother exhibits wistful and loving emotions—indicating the she can identify with her daughter, naturalizing the feminine response to romance. It is in this moment that the heterogendered division of labor becomes visible. The audience learns through these interactions that "falling in love" with the "right" man is what makes marriage desirable and necessary. These instances in popular culture teach us that what counts as "marriage" is compliance with tradition, patriarchy, and the heterogendered social order. It is unimaginable to have feelings of love and desire for commitment without investing in marriage and the expensive white wedding.

"Tell Him That You Care Just for Him, Do the Things He Likes to Do . . ."

In the movie *My Best Friend's Wedding*, Julianne's (Julia Roberts) best friend Michael (Dermot Mulroney) announces he will marry Kimmy (Cameron Diaz). Kimmy is a young, blond, blue-eyed daughter of a very rich man who owns a cable sports network, the ultimate masculine fantasy. Because of her class standing, she has all the opportunities for an education and career befitting someone of her socioeconomic background. Michael is a lower-middle-class sports writer who lives on hot dogs, travels all over the country covering baseball, and sleeps in cheap motels but loves his job. As the story line develops we learn that Julianne, a nationally syndicated food critic, wants to get Michael to marry her instead of Kimmy, and she sets out to win the competition for Michael's love and commitment. The film contrasts the two women, characterizing them as polar opposites, where one, Kimmy, is desirable because she is traditionally feminine, while the other, Julianne, is destined for a life of career without love. At one point in the movie, Kimmy explains to Julianne why she will give up her plans to finish college and law school to travel with Michael and allow him to continue the work he loves so much. "It's his career! I'm supportive. I want to be with the man I love. I can always go to school, but I can't always be with the man I love." After inviting Julianne to be maid of honor, Kimmy takes her to a bridal salon to select a bridesmaid's gown. During the fitting, while Julianne is up on a pedestal being attended to by a seamstress, the following exchange occurs:

> Kimmy: You wouldn't be comfortable unless you were distinctive.
> Julianne: What else did he tell you?
> Kimmy: You hate weddings, you never go. You're not up for anything conventional or that's assumed to be a female priority, including marriage, romance, or even . . .
> Julianne: . . . love?! Michael and I were a wrong fit right from the start.
> Kimmy: He said that too. Well, I thought I was like you . . . and proud to be. But, then I met rumpled, smelly old Michael! And I found out I was a sentimental schmuck like all those flighty nitwits I'd always pitied. It's funny huh?

The film sets up a competition between the new woman and the traditional woman of the 1990s, in which the outcome is predictable. The woman who is "sentimental" will join all those "flighty nitwits"—who must not have been so dumb after all—and will become the winner in this feminine competition. The woman who yields to romance and domestic priorities over those of career and profession is the one who will be the bride. The loser, Julianne, will always be just "the bridesmaid." This construction of the bridesmaid parallels depictions in other sites in popular culture, like the black bridesmaids in *Bride's* magazine, signaling to the new woman that she is living on the edge of acceptability if she does not submit to her feminine position in this heterogendered, capitalist social order.

The linkage of patriarchal heterosexuality with capitalism is in evidence in this story. Historically, the need to recruit women into the professional-managerial class is increasing, providing women with greater economic independence from men while serving the needs of capitalism. Meanwhile, while the economic need for women to marry a male "breadwinner" is decreasing, the material necessity of marriage is in decline. To maintain a heterogendered division of labor that serves the interests of patriarchal heterosexuality as well as the wedding-industrial complex, the wedding-ideological complex is producing a variety of messages to entice women to continue to marry. By providing images and messages that construct romantic love and the heterogendered division of labor as the "natural order" of things, the continuation of marriage and of patriarchal relations of production that subordinate women's interests to men's power is secured.

The conclusion of this competitive exchange between these two characters takes place in an elevator, where Kimmy tells Julianne she "wins." When Julianne asks what she means, Kimmy responds: "He's got you on a pedestal and me in his arms." For Kimmy, that's the ultimate marker of romantic success. As Julianne and Kimmy exit the elevator and enter a family gathering, a young woman exclaims: "Look! It's the bride and the woman she'll never live up to!" Ideologically, this film conveys the message that even though "he" finds the professional, ambitious career woman attractive and compelling, his interest in her will succumb to the desire for a woman who adheres to the heterogender codes of femininity, placing his needs above her own.

In addition to the issues of heterogender, class, and accumulation in this film, other dominant ideologies concerning difference are evident. Once again, the all-white cast combined with the linkage of wealth and wedding, much like the images in bridal and celebrity wedding magazines, signals to the viewer that weddings are code for whiteness. It should be evident by now that weddings in popular culture are sites where the structured invisibility of whiteness and its normative privileges are continually reproduced. If we look at weddings "head-on," we see their true role in our culture.

Another increasingly popular ideological strategy in *My Best Friend's Wedding* is the use of a gay character to secure the heterosexual imaginary. Julianne's closest friend, outside of Michael, is George (Rupert Everett), her editor. As she plots to get Michael back, George plays her confidante, her guy/girlfriend. He does the affective work typically assigned to women, helping her sort through her feelings and comforting and caring for her when she is distraught. George urges her to tell Michael she's still in love with him. When she loses her nerve, she declares that George is her fiancé, in the hope that Michael will discover his jealousy and leave

Kimmy. What follows is a charade, in which George pretends to be heterosexual and madly in love with Julianne. At one point, Michael questions this news by saying he thought Julianne had told him George was gay. They all laugh, and George denies that he is and says that sometimes he pretends he is. The personhood of George is erased in this moment, when he is called upon to lie about his very identity—a moment that is a not-so-subtle act of gay bashing. Of course, the taken-for-granted fact here is that if even the gay guy can trivialize and subordinate himself to preserve the interests of the heterosexual imaginary, then so can we the audience. In keeping with the wedding-ideological complex, this makes perfect sense: gay people must be erased in order for heterosexuality to maintain its dominance.

In a hilarious scene in the movie, George and Julianne must pose as a couple during a lunch with Kimmy's family and Michael. Seated at a large table in a very busy restaurant, George is asked how he and Julianne met and fell in love. To answer their questions, George sings:

> The moment I wake up
> Before I put on my makeup
> I say a little prayer for you.
> . . . Forever and ever, I'll stay in your heart
> oh how I love you,
> together forever, we never will part.

Everyone is tickled to hear him be so romantic, and they soon join George in singing the entire song, celebrating their romance and engagement. Julianne is less than pleased that George may have foiled her plan by being too demonstrative—that is, too gay—and eventually tells Michael that she's not engaged.

The film ends with Michael's and Kimmy's big white wedding complete with white Rolls Royce and firework sprays lining the driveway as Julianne must face the loss of her potential love partner. Once again, George, who apparently has no life of his own, comes to the rescue, appearing at the wedding reception complete with tuxedo and prepared to dance the night away with Julianne.

The use of the gay character as cipher in the service of heterosexuality is a theme prevalent in many films and television shows. As battles over the legitimacy of homosexuality and human rights for gays, lesbians, and bisexuals are fought out in a wide variety of political arenas today, the contradictory use of gay characters speaks to a state of ambivalence about the institution of heterosexuality and the legitimacy of homosexuality. This recent trend in popular film and television weddings is to make use of gays and lesbians to both provide a broader audience appeal—marketing to gays and lesbians—and to target a potential wedding market should legal weddings for same-sex couples ever be allowed. The abuse of gay characters serves the interests of heterosexual supremacy and also provides some comfort for those who claim opposition to homosexuality, e.g., the Disney boycott by the religious right mentioned earlier. The question that arises from these patterns is: What are the social consequences of these portrayals of gay men and lesbians?

This theme of the gay male with the heterosexual woman has become enormously popular with the success of this movie, a subsequent film, *Object of My Affection*, and the new NBC television show *Will & Grace*, where the lead characters are a heterosexual woman and a gay man who are also best friends and roommates.

These examples are successful on two levels. First, they provide the heterosexual female viewer with the ultimate romantic fantasy of the perfect man. Not only is he handsome and desirable, he's loving, emotional, caring, and sensitive, traits that are hard to find among heterosexual men. The only drawback in these otherwise perfect male/female relationships is the absence of sexual attraction on his part. But it is this "lack" that produces the popularity of these shows. The audience, firmly situated in the heterosexual imaginary, is unable to suspend their belief that men are "naturally" attracted to women. Secretly, they hope he will "come to his senses" and consummate a heterosexual union. Interestingly, the use of the gay male as guy/girlfriend resecures the patriarchal order by erasing the heterosexual woman's need for a female friend while creating a space for the possibility of a masculine man as a love interest. In the end, the institution of heterosexuality is preserved as dominant and superior because, by contrast, it appears stable and less confusing.

"They're Writing Songs of Love, but Not for Me . . . "

Similar to the two films discussed thus far, *Four Weddings and a Funeral* makes use of the intersection of the ideology of romantic love and the ideology of hetero-gender. This British romantic comedy, which experienced enormous box office success in the U.S., tells the story of Charles (Hugh Grant), a twenty-something white man, and his cohort of friends caught in the flurry of weddings the film portrays as prevalent among people in their twenties.

The movie follows the love story of Charles and Carrie (Andie McDowell), the American woman he falls in love with at the first wedding in the film, in a classic case of poor timing. They meet at the first wedding, are attracted to each other, and spend the night together. The following morning, when he discovers she must leave for the U.S. immediately, they both express their disappointment at a lost opportunity. He encounters her again at the second wedding, only this time she introduces Charles to her wealthy fiancé. Charles is devastated and confesses to his friends that he is in love for the first time in his life. He receives an invitation to Carrie's wedding and, in a serendipitous meeting when Charles checks in on Carrie's bridal registry, confesses to her that he loves her. The third wedding is Carrie's. While momentous to Charles given his romantic interest in Carrie, it is at this wedding that Gareth, one of Charles's friends, dies of a heart attack. Charles encounters Carrie at the funeral and doesn't see her again until his own wedding day. Rather than risk life without marriage, and with his true love married to someone else, Charles decides to settle and marry someone he believes he loves enough. Carrie appears at the wedding, reveals she is divorced, and the fourth wedding becomes the movie's crisis point. Charles publicly declares his love for Carrie and destroys the wedding. The film concludes with Carrie and Charles reunited and committed to each other but not to marriage.

One of the central themes of this film is what counts as true love. Charles, his friends Thomas, Fiona, Gareth, Matthew, and Charlotte, and his deaf brother David travel from wedding to wedding ruminating about whether they will ever find someone to marry. As we witness Charles experience "love at first sight" with Carrie, as well as subsequent interactions among the other main characters in their quest to find a spouse, we learn that true love and romance are first and foremost about appearances and chemistry. At each wedding, there is reference to someone as "quite attractive," "a dish," or "lovely" when sizing up potential love partners. Interestingly, nowhere in this film is there any reference to what these characters do for a living, if anything, or to what else they care about in life. According to this film, one need only find someone—of the opposite sex—attractive in order to find them suitable for marriage.

The defining moment of the film is when Charles and Thomas go for a walk after Gareth's funeral. At the service, Matthew delivers a very moving eulogy using a poem by gay poet W. H. Auden, revealing how much he and Gareth loved each other.

> . . . he was my north, my south, my east and west,
> my working week and my Sunday's rest,
> my noon, my midnight, my talk, my song.
> I thought that love would last forever . . .

To the surprise of all of their friends and to the viewers who watched Gareth and Matthew participate as single men in each of the weddings, it is revealed that, in fact, what they've all been searching for was under their noses all the time. As Charles reflects: "It's odd isn't it? All these years we've been single and proud of it, two of us were for all intents and purposes married all this time." In an interesting twist, the heterosexual imaginary in this film depends upon the love shared by two men. Never is the question posed as to why these two men who were obviously in a committed relationship "passed" for single and heterosexual. Never do any of their "friends" act concerned about why Gareth and Matthew couldn't be open with them. This gay relationship is used throughout the movie to legitimize and justify institutionalized heterosexuality. Gareth and Matthew are always portrayed as celebratory of heterosexual marriage and as key supporters of weddings. It takes the tragedy of Gareth's death and the revelation of their "closeted" love, cloaked in the guise of single heterosexuality, to teach the main characters as well as the viewer what married love is really all about.

Charles: Thomas, one thing I find really . . . uh . . . it's your total
confidence that will get married. What if you never find the right girl?
Thomas: Sorry?
Charles: Surely if that service shows anything, it shows that there is
such a thing as a perfect match. If we can't be like Gareth and
Matthew, then, maybe we should just let it go. Some of us are not
going to get married.
Thomas: Well, I don't know, Charlie. The truth is, unlike you, I never
expected the thunder bolt. I'd always just hoped I'd meet some nice
friendly girl, like the look of her, hope that the look of me didn't make
her physically sick, and pop the question, and settle down and be
happy.
Charles: Yeah, maybe you're right. Maybe all this waiting for one true
love stuff gets you no where.

The tension of these two positions is evident throughout the film. Should you
marry someone you like well enough to share a life with or should you wait for your
"one true love"—or as Thomas says, the "thunder bolt?" Throughout the movie
Thomas is portrayed as a homely, clumsy, bumbling, boring, but wealthy nerd.
Charles, on the other hand, is a glib, attractive, sexy, charming, committed bachelor. To embody the "settling for love" position in the character of Thomas creates
an association between the character and the position. The film's success depends
upon the linkage of "real" romantic love with the handsome and desirable leading
man. The "break" the failed wedding represents secures this position, signaling to
the viewer the necessity and glory of true heterosexual romantic love while preserving the need for the white wedding.

Another important feature of this film is the way it uses class and the ideology
of accumulation to secure the heterosexual imaginary. All of the weddings in the
film are extravagant, large, white weddings with brides in white wedding gowns
and veils. The ceremonies and vows are all traditionally Anglican, and the churches are all large and ornate. In each instance the viewer is left with the impression

that the bride and groom are at least upper middle class and more than likely wealthy. Thomas's family is the seventh richest in England, residing in a 137-room castle. Carrie's first marriage is to an extremely wealthy Scot.

The only breaks in the upper-class trappings are at the funeral, which is set in a drab, working-class neighborhood, and at the end, when we get a brief glimpse of Charles's modest middle-class urban flat which he shares with his roommate, Charlotte. Notably, the only two rainy scenes are at the funeral and during the conclusion when Charles and Carrie reunite. In the funeral scene the signifiers attached to gay love and death are of gloom and destitution, while the closing scene transforms the gloom of rain with higher-class surroundings and a symbolic thunder bolt.

During the credits, snapshots of each of the main characters are shown, providing the viewer with the requisite happy ending. Except for Charles and Carrie, each character, including Thomas, is shown wedding their true love. Even Matthew, the remaining gay friend, is shown having some sort of coupling celebration with another man. In the end, while this film allows for an alternative and resistance, neither option is as attractive as the white wedding. The ideology of heterosexual supremacy is secured by rendering same-sex love meaningful but dismal.

Similar patterns are used in wedding episodes on *Suddenly Susan* and *Ellen*. In both instances, gay men are used to celebrate the traditional white heterosexual wedding. In *Suddenly Susan*, Vicki wants to marry a rabbi but doesn't have the money for a big white wedding. Two gay male coworkers who are planning a $50,000 wedding for themselves invite Vicki to have a double wedding with them so she won't miss out on all the class trappings of the big white wedding. She accepts. The portrayal of the gay men is flat, with no affection, dancing, or kissing between the two men. Vicki, on the other hand, is at center stage as the white bride with the white wedding gown and the charismatic and handsome rabbi in tow. There is no question that the "real" wedding and the only one of any interest to the viewer is Vicki's.

In an earlier episode of the now-canceled *Ellen* show, Paige is going to wed Matt,

Thomas: "At least it's one we won't forget. I mean a lot of weddings just blend in to each other, don't they?"

—Four Weddings and a Funeral (1993)

a handsome, white police officer. The traditional trappings are in place with one small exception. Ellen as maid of honor is dressed in a pale-blue pants suit. While everyone is waiting for the ceremony to start, Ellen discovers Paige in her wedding dress engaged in a passionate embrace with Spence, Ellen's roommate. After some confrontation Paige reveals that she and Spence have been attracted to each other for a while. Ellen, taking her job as maid of honor very seriously, frantically attempts to pacify the wedding guests while Paige works things out with the groom-to-be. Sitting at a piano in the front of the church Ellen starts to serenade the guests with the song "Heart and Soul." Within a couple of bars, her two gay male friends Peter and Barrett burst into song with Ellen and help her save the wedding from disaster. At one point, Peter exclaims: "Guilty! I love weddings! My father was a wedding coordinator so I guess it's in my blood! Princess Di's was like the moon landing for me." As the audience roars at the absurdity of this, it's clear that gay men can participate in these ceremonies and be acceptable provided they serve as comic relief and both celebrate and appreciate heterosexual weddings. Obscured from view in these displays of heterosexual supremacy is the humanity of gays and lesbians. Historically, heterosexual weddings are frequently painful experiences for gays and lesbians, who are often cast in support/cheerleader roles while their own relationships are trivialized and ignored. As the buffoons or effeminate clowns who "love weddings," gay men are used as a site for ridicule, contributing to the social conditions that legitimize anti-gay discrimination and violence.

"It's a Nice Day for a White Wedding . . ."

The Wedding Singer is a campy romantic comedy full of garish colors and unusual-looking people. This film makes use of dominant notions of difference to legitimize romantic love, a heterogendered division of labor, and marriage. Robbie Hart (Adam Sandler) is the wedding singer, performing at working-class to lower-middle-class weddings in a small town where all of the receptions are held at the same banquet hall. Portrayed as a very sweet, considerate guy, Robbie meets Julia (Drew Barrymore), one of the waitresses where he's singing. In their first conversation they tell each other about their engagements and wedding plans. Robbie tells Julia he is getting married next week, and Julia tells Robbie that her boyfriend, Glen, won't set a date.

In the next scene, we watch as Robbie is stood up at the altar, when Linda changes her mind about marrying Robbie and doesn't appear for their formal white wedding. Humiliated in front of half the town, Robbie finds out from Linda that she decided she didn't want to be married to a wedding singer and stay in Ridgefield for the rest of her life. At this point in the film, we learn that Robbie is a nice, small-town guy who cares about kids, old ladies, and being romantic.

Julia, a small, big-eyed blond, who dresses sweetly and is kind to everyone, is engaged to Glen (Matthew Glave), a smooth-talking, handsome financial analyst who loves to womanize, talk big, and bully gentle guys like Robbie. In a sense, this film works more like a cartoon than a movie, setting Glen and Linda up as the "bad guys" and Robbie and Julia—a '90s Romeo and Juliet—as the "good guys," who are obviously meant to be together because they have so much in common. Before we reach the predictable romantic happy ending, in which Robbie defeats Glen for Julia's love, we learn through constructions of difference what makes people worthy of marriage.

Robbie's band is made up of three performers. His backup singer is a Boy George lookalike named George. Whenever he's left to fill in for Robbie he sings Boy George's song "Do You Really Want to Hurt Me?" In each instance we watch as the wedding guests get more and more abusive and disgusted by this cross-dressing, gender-bending guy. The humor at this point depends on the audience finding this Boy George "wannabe," coded as stereotypically gay, repulsive and laughable, and the violence of the wedding guests understandable. At several points throughout the movie there are mocking references to gays or homoerotic behaviors. Even Robbie is constructed as having gay behaviors. In several scenes between Robbie and Glen, "the bully," Glen, makes reference to Robbie as "limp-wristed" or effeminate because he's considerate and gentle.

In his first public appearance following his "jilting," Robbie is consumed with emotion and enraged at the prospect that he's not going to marry. It doesn't really matter that he's lost Linda. What's really important is that he believes no one else will want him, that he's not worthy of marriage. To make his point he sings the song "Love Stinks" and invites another marriage reject, a fat man, to sing the song with him. During this sequence Robbie identifies for the audience which people will never marry:

> Some of us will never ever find true love. Take for instance . . . me! And take, for instance, that guy right there. And that lady with the sideburns and, basically, everybody at table 9. And the interesting thing is . . . me, fatty, the lady with the sideburns, and the mutants at table 9 will never ever find a way to better our situation, because apparently we have absolutely nothing to offer the opposite sex.

In this amazing scene, Robbie identifies all the unfit people in the room and declares that neither he nor any of them are marriageable. No one would want anyone that ugly, useless, and undesirable. This is designed to be one of the most humorous segments in the film, inviting the audience to join Robbie in agreeing that these people are undesirable. In the climax of this scene Robbie moves around the reception inviting each of the "mutants" to join him in singing "Love Stinks." For the first time during the wedding reception, they smile and become excited. The scene ends with the father of the bride punching Robbie.

These constructions of difference act as social control mechanisms, elevating the institution of heterosexuality and weddings by coding those who don't marry as deviant, ugly, unworthy, and resentful. By contrast, those who marry and have the traditional white wedding are constructed as superior. Their joy in singing "Love Stinks" only reinforces the pattern that anyone who doesn't enjoy a wedding or who acknowledges the pain of so-called love relationships is predictably bitter and resentful because they're unfit. The blame for being without a partner or without love is placed firmly on the shoulders of the individual who's not worthy rather than on a culture that sets up these social arrangements and their corresponding social controls.

A similar pattern occurs in the *Lois & Clark* television wedding where Superman marries Lois Lane. A villain called the "wedding destroyer" attempts to murder Lois at the altar to force Clark to live with the type of pain she's had to endure since her groom-to-be died on his way to their wedding. Ideologically, these messages work to demonstrate that anyone who would dislikes weddings is either disfigured or hostile.

The boundaries of acceptability are clearly demarcated in both of these examples, establishing what counts as beautiful, attractive, desirable, and worthy of love and marriage by making visible what typifies the opposite of these things as well as the consequences of occupying these marginalized positions.

In addition to ideologies of difference, *The Wedding Singer* also establishes that weddings and wedding preparations are the space of the feminine and the domain of women, that dreams are made of finding true love, and that happiness can be found by a woman surrendering her identity to the right man. As Julia prepares for her wedding, she tries on her white wedding gown and stands in front of the mirror and rehearses what she will say in the receiving line.

> Hi, nice to meet you. I'm Mrs. Glen Gulia. I'm Julia Gulia.
>
> It's nice to meet you, I'm Mrs. Julia Gulia [she sobs].
>
> Hi, I'm Mrs. Robbie Hart. Robbie and I are so pleased you could come to our wedding [she beams].

In this moment Julia realizes she loves Robbie but believes she has to go through with the wedding because she thinks Robbie is back with Linda. Robbie finds out Julia and Glen are on their way to Las Vegas to get married and follows her there. Much to his surprise, he realizes they're on the same plane. He finds her while Glen is in the bathroom, sings a romantic song he wrote for her, and they declare their love for each other. Boy meets girl, boy gets girl . . . and the scene ends with a kiss in front of everyone on the plane as they applaud. The conclusion of the film is—you guessed it!—a big white wedding. The ideology of romantic love overcomes all obstacles except those it keeps in place to preserve the interests of patriarchal capitalism and the institution of heterosexuality.

"We Are Family . . . I've Got All My Sisters and Me . . ."

The Birdcage is a remake of the famous French film *La Cage aux Folles,* popular in the 1970s. Armand Goldman (Robin Williams) and Albert (Nathan Lane) are a gay couple who own a gay nightclub in Miami. Their son, Val (Dan Futterman), comes home from college to announce he is getting married to Barbara (Calista Flockhart), the daughter of ultraconservative Senator Keeley (Gene Hackman) and Mrs. Keeley (Dianne Wiest).

After breaking the news of the marriage, Val tells Armand and Albert that the Keeleys will be coming to dinner the next day. He also tells them that the Keeleys think Val's parents are heterosexual and that Armand is a diplomat. What follows is an elaborate charade to provide Val with the trappings of the upstanding—white, upper-middle-class—heterosexual family in order to protect his chance to marry Barbara.

Just as in *In & Out* where the gay character attempts to learn how to be more masculine, as similar scenario is played out in this film. Albert, who is transgendered and a female impersonator of some renown, tries to learn how to be masculine. What's important about these scenes in both films is how they demonstrate the arbitrary and constructed nature of gender while suggesting that it's difficult to overcome nature. Albert fails miserably and, instead, decides to dress as a conservative, middle-aged woman and pretend to be Armand's wife.

Once again, we see a film made in the late 1990s that makes use of gay characters to portray a heterosexual romantic comedy. There are several scenes in *The Birdcage* that work to erase the identities of the gay men. One in particular is the lie perpetrated by their own son, who asks his parents to deny their sexuality and love for each other. Instead, he wants them to pretend to be both heterosexual and from a different social class. Val adds insult to injury when he asks if Albert can be sent away for the evening and if his real mother (Val is the result of a one-night stand Armand had in his twenties) can come and pretend to be married to Armand. The violence this inflicts upon the two people who've raised Val is translated into humor. The humor in this passage depends upon the audience seeing the ridiculousness of this gay couple, especially in relation to the sanctity of "the wedding."

As long as the audience can laugh at these scenes, they don't have to see the humanity of gays or lesbians or take their lives and families seriously.

Senator Keeley has agreed to this wedding to "whitewash" a sex scandal involving his close legislative associate. Of note here, the sex scandal involved an underage African-American woman, only one of two instances where a person of color has any role in this film. By this point in the story, the message to the audience is that both sets of parents live on the margins of acceptability. Val and Barbara, by contrast, appear moderate, stable, rational, and moral, the very model of upstanding heterosexuality and worthy of an elegant white wedding.

The heterosexual imaginary working in this film makes use of the ideology of difference, relegating the gay family to the level of the absurd, constructing the Latino houseboy as silly and stupid, and playing on the racist stereotype of the oversexed black teenager in the depiction of the scandal. All of these examples secure the audience's belief in the stability and superiority of the heterosexual white center of American society. The association of the wealthy diplomat with the values of the ultraconservative senator works to link wealth and accumulation with decency, morality, and "family values."

The story turns when all is revealed. Val claims his love and pride in his parents, and the Keeleys attempt to call off the wedding. The saving moment emerges when the paparazzi surround the building and the senator has to rely on Armand and Albert to help him escape. They dress all of them in "drag" and hurry them out through the crowd in the nightclub. The final scene of the movie is—you guessed it again! A big extravagant white wedding!

"You Were Meant for Me, and I Was Meant for You . . ."

Object of My Affection is not a wedding film in that a wedding is not the central theme, but a wedding is the setting for the turning point in the story. Integral to the new trend in popular culture to pair the heterosexual woman with gay man, *Object of My Affection* keeps company with *My Best Friend's Wedding* and *Will & Grace*, and in some ways sets the standard for this genre.

Nina saves George from homelessness when his male lover "dumps" him for a new relationship. Even though Nina has a boyfriend and is pregnant, before long she falls in love with George. Their friendship walks the line on closeness, with both loving each other intensely but not sexually. They take ballroom dancing lessons together to varying versions of "You Were Meant for Me." Before long, she realizes she has a better relationship with George and breaks off her relationship with her boyfriend, Vince. She wants to create a family with George, who is more than willing to comply. The crisis comes when George falls in love with Paul, bringing home the reality that he is, in fact, gay.

The tension in this movie depends upon the audience believing that a gay man just hasn't met the right woman yet. Throughout the movie, it's clear that George has indeed met the right woman but it doesn't make any difference. He's still gay! Ideologically, this film explores a range of alternatives to the white heterosexual nuclear family but, in the end, upholds the centrality of institutionalized heterosexuality with a twist.

George invites Nina to his brother's wedding. In a scene at another big white wedding, Nina confronts George about his feelings for her. George mistakes her emotions for late-term pregnancy strain:

> George: Weddings can be a little much.
> Nina: But it works.
> George: What do you mean?
> Nina: I was watching Frank and Caroline today and I just kept thinking. . . . This is real . . . and George and I are not.
> George: We're just different.
> Nina: But I don't think that I am that different. I want you to be with me. I want you to marry me. I want you to love me the way that I love you. I don't really want to see who you are at all.
> George: I think you see me.
> Nina: Then tell me the truth. What do you want?
> George: I want Paul.
> Nina: I know . . . you can't choose who you love.

There are several important things about this passage. In it Nina acknowledges that her romantic feelings keep her from seeing reality—who George is. It also affirms the white wedding as the standard-bearer for what counts as "real" even in the face of the heterosexual imaginary. The song "You Were Meant for Me" plays at significant moments in the film, naturalizing the connection between George and Nina but suggesting that, in the end, if you can't overcome nature, there are some alternatives that will uphold the institution of heterosexuality as dominant and superior. Ironically, George and Nina are the same names of the parents in *Father of the Bride,* leading us to wonder if the sequel to this "new family" film will be the wedding of their daughter. The film concludes with Nina partnered with an African-American police officer, George with Paul, and the baby being raised by all of them. The first time I saw this movie was in a moderately crowded theater. At the point in the above dialogue where George says he "wants" Paul, the audience rippled with exclamations of disbelief. Behind me a young man exclaimed, "What?" "Huh?" Even when confronted with the obvious, the heterosexual imaginary is a powerful force.

Following this model, in the television sitcom *Will & Grace,* Will and Grace become roommates after Grace leaves her fiancé at the altar. When she realizes that she is closer to Will, the wedding no longer makes sense. She and Will call each other best friends and decide to live together. Everything they do together simulates what it means to be an intimate heterosexual couple, except for having sex. This new category—"all-but-married" or ABM—preserves the interests of heterosexuality but confirms the "naturalness" of men and women being together even if they're not sexually involved. Friends and coworkers continually remark that they act like a married couple. Whenever Will seems interested in meeting a man, Grace somehow foils his attempt. Where this show will go remains to be seen, but the pattern of casting gay male characters with heterosexual women shows signs of continuing.

Considering the cancellation of *Ellen* for being too openly lesbian, this trend seems somewhat contradictory. However, it's important to recognize the interests at stake here. The success of the ABM model depends upon the circulation of the heterosexual imaginary making it possible for the audience to desire some form of heterosexual resolution. Maybe Will will will away his gay self in favor of grace-ful heterosexual coupling with Grace. *Ellen* did not provide this option. It offered the ultimate radical break, the joining of two women in a patriarchal society that "needs" women to "need" men.

Significantly, the market the media are seeking is largely female, young, and consumption oriented. Given the recent marketing analyses of gays and lesbians, it is evident that gay men are also big spenders, adding to the market reach of a show that draws in white women and gay men. This new genre appeals to both markets and attempts to capitalize on their interests while preserving the sanctity of heterosexual supremacy.

"Wishin' and Hopin' and Thinkin' and Prayin', Plannin' and Dreamin' . . ."

In several television situation comedies the importance of the wedding gown and the dream of a white wedding are dominant themes for female characters. Revealed in these episodes are patterns pertaining to the naturalization of wed-dings as integral to being a woman. As Sally in *Third Rock from the Sun* says in response to Dick's query about why she agreed to get married, Sally explains, "I'm a woman and he asked me. That's what women are supposed to do." Even an alien from another galaxy can see the significance of the wedding and marriage to women's identity. Sally also realizes what cultural capital weddings provide when, upon agreeing to marry a man in need of a green card, she proclaims, "Finally, I have something I can lord over other women!" It's not simply a matter of feminine duty, it is also a measure of a woman's worth in patriarchal heterosexual culture and shows her allegiance to patriarchal priorities.

Everyone Loves Raymond is a situation comedy about the issues a lower-middle-class couple with three young children face with their family, Ray's parents, and his single brother. In two recent episodes of *Raymond*, Ray and his wife, Debra, reminisce about their wedding. When Raymond proposed marriage to Debra, sev-eral mishaps occurred. To make sure Debra really said yes, Raymond went to her apartment, presented her with a diamond, and asked her all over again if she would marry him. She grabbed the ring, began screaming, and jumped up and down for joy, spinning around the room. Ray still was not convinced that Debra was saying yes to him. He pulled the diamond away from her and asked her again. Finally, she said yes in a way he thought he could believe. When he gave her back the diamond, she began squealing all over again, giving Ray the impression that what she was saying yes to was the ring. Once she calmed down, Debra called Ray to the couch to show him her plans. "I've got to show you all my plans. . . . I've been planning this since I was twelve." It turns out Debra has a box full of wedding-planning materials she's been saving for years. Ray remarks that they've only known each other for three months, and wonders how she could have been planning this wedding since she was twelve. At that moment there's a knock on the door, and Debra's parents come in. They've confirmed the country club for the reception. Even though she tells Raymond she wants to have a small wedding, it quickly becomes clear that small for Debra is 200–250 people, affirming the average (natural) expenditure of $19,000 on a white wedding. As Debra and her mother share dream plans for the wedding, Raymond wonders if he even needs to come. Debra exclaims: "It's the happiest day of our lives!" Once again, the commodification of the wedding and the heterosexual imaginary are secured. How can anyone refuse to participate in the happiest day a woman has been planning since she was a small child? For women, the message is clear. Anything women do or achieve pales in comparison to the moment of the wedding. Happiness, contingent upon such an event in her life, is the ultimate goal, regardless of its costs to the people involved or to the race, class, gender, sexuality, and labor conditions it depends upon and preserves.

This same theme presents itself in the recent *Friends* wedding of Ross and Emily. In one pre-wedding episode, Emily asks Ross's sister Monica to pick up her wedding gown at the bridal shop. Monica agrees, goes to the store, and, mistaken for Emily, tries on the wedding gown. In the next scene, we see the sales woman telling Monica the store is now closing, giving the viewer the impression that Monica has been there most of the day. This dress is so important, Monica has given up an entire day just to try one on. She brings the gown home and wears it while doing the dishes. When Phoebe arrives and appears scandalized that Monica is wearing the gown, Monica explains how good it feels. "You should try it!" she exclaims. In the next scene both Phoebe and Monica are walking around in wedding gowns talking about how good it feels to wear one. When Rachel arrives and is feeling depressed, Phoebe and Monica tell her about the "gown thing" saying, "We've got something that will make you feel better!" In the next scene, all three women are sitting on the couch in wedding gowns, eating popcorn and talking about how uplifting it is to wear a wedding gown. These are women whose lives are thus far incomplete. They haven't found a man to marry yet, and the gowns comfort them with the promise of good things to come and the soothing feeling being feminine and beautiful brings. They can't see each other as valuable and can't talk to each other about anything but men, love, and romance.

The wedding of Ross and Emily takes place in London. When they all arrive there, Ross and Emily go to the church to see how things will be set up, only to find that the wrecking ball has taken away the better part of the building. Emily, in tears, says the wedding is off. Ross sees this as ridiculous given that so many people have flown to England for the wedding. In a scene with his sister, Monica, he angrily exclaims that calling off the wedding is really stupid. Monica responds:

> Monica: How long have you been planning this wedding?
> Ross: A month.
> Monica: Emily's probably been planning this since she was five, ever since the first time she took a pillowcase and hung it off the back of her head. That's what we did! We dreamed about the perfect wedding and the perfect place with the perfect four-tiered wedding cake with the little people on top. And, we had the perfect guy who understood why this is important to us.

Without question, these scenes from several situation comedies illustrate the pervasiveness of messages naturalizing white weddings as both the woman's domain and as central to her sense of herself.

These themes are pervasive in popular culture, signaling a disturbing trend among the white middle class—the nearly exclusive obsession of young white women with romance and weddings. Without exception, it appears that this is all women think or care about. The consequence to women can be profound, manifesting in a form of anti-intellectualism where women are concerned, reducing their expectations in life to one moment of spectacle, rendering their talents and desires to the domestic sphere, trivializing their interests in the world around them, and situating them as the standard-bearers of traditional femininity and the heterogendered division of labor.

The heterogendered division of labor and heterosexual supremacy are well preserved in television and popular film, inviting us to laugh and cry while we celebrate the setbacks and triumphs of characters who appear real to us. As we do, we become complicit in the ways of thinking that allow for racial, class, gender, and sexual hierarchies, varying kinds of sexual/gender violence, a patriarchal heterogendered division of labor, and subservience to a class/accumulation model for personal relations. The heterosexual imaginary circulating in popular film and television works to obscure these consequences by cloaking them in humor and romance. And it discourages any critical analysis of the consequences of how we've organized and regulated heterosexuality as an institution. In the end, we're left to wonder who it is, exactly, who lives "happily ever after."

Chapter Five

And They Lived Happily Ever After . . .

"... the Defense of Marriage Act–will safeguard the sacred institutions of marriage and the family from those who seek to destroy them and who are willing to tear apart America's moral fabric in the process."

Jesse Helms, Senate, September 9, 1996

"... white people's conscious racialization of others does not necessarily lead to a conscious racialization of the white self.... [W]hiteness makes itself invisible precisely by asserting its normalcy, its transparency, in contrast with the marking of others on which its transparency depends.... [H]ow whiteness is seen is anything but random: rather, it can be accounted for, analyzed, and challenged."

Ruth Frankenberg, Displacing Whiteness

"They [homosexuals] start by pretending that it is just another form of love. It's sickening."

Jesse Helms, Congressional Quarterly, 1996

"There's no longer the subordinate status of women to the extent there was in earlier eras–there is simply too much freedom and money sloshing around. We may be heading into what some sociologists call a 'postmarriage society,' where women will raise the children and men will not be there in any stable, institutional way. If so, we'd better build more prisons."

spokesman for the Institute for American Values to Stephanie Coontz, The Way We Really Are

Once upon a time, in a land far, far away, a handsome prince met a beautiful maiden, swept her off her feet, married her in a perfect white wedding ceremony, and carried her away to a land of fairy tales and dreams where they raised three gorgeous children and lived happily ever after. This is the dominant romantic fairy-tale story line. Following this formula, the last chapter in this story of white weddings is the place where I'm supposed to smooth out rough edges, tie up loose ends, and resolve any conflicts and contradictions from the preceding pages. It's also the point where I'm expected to comfort the reader by offering examples of exceptions to these practices, tales of resistance, and alternatives to the dominant form. I'm supposed to say "I know *your* wedding was (or will be) different" or "I'm sure *your* wedding didn't (or won't) participate in these patterns." In other words, it's time to keep this romance, this securing of the heterosexual imaginary, going by providing the happy ending to this wedding story. Were I to remain critical of the institution of heterosexuality and deny the reader some form of redemption, the social controls that work to suppress wedding resisters would activate. To develop critical consciousness when romance is the prevailing form is to challenge the boundaries of acceptability. To explain my critique the reader could construct me as unfit for marriage, embittered by love lost, or just not a very happy person. This is the heterosexual imaginary at work, securing the interests of the institution of patriarchal heterosexuality under late capitalism and its wedding-industrial complex.

Examining the social and material conditions upon which white weddings depend does not allow for a happy ending. The consequences of many of the practices associated with white weddings, the wedding-industrial complex, and the wedding-ideological complex are disturbing and unsettling. In a society filled with various types of fairy tales and romance, e.g., love, sports, and religion, it's sometimes difficult to see our real conditions of existence, let alone attend to the hardships and inequities they produce, the ways we are implicated in these problems, and the powerful interests they serve.

Viewing the various sites in popular culture where images and messages concerning white weddings dominate, it becomes clear that the intended audience is women, particularly white women, and that weddings are the domain of the feminine. More importantly, examining all of these sites together reveals the extent to which the dominant social order seeks to produce feminine subjects whose very existence and identity is organized by the ideology of romantic love. In addition to gaining consent to the heterogendered division of labor where women are responsible for and provide unpaid domestic and affective labor, the less obvious outcome is the privileging of romance discourse in women's everyday lives.

As a teacher, I learned some time ago that if you want to get the attention of your students you need only mention the word "sex." Considering the findings of this study on weddings, I discovered that the use of the word "romance" among women has much the same effect. In fact, it is a topic about which many young women obsess. "Will I find 'the one,' 'my one true love,' 'the love of my life?'" "Am I attractive or worthy enough?" "Can I make this person happy enough to stay with me?" Or, worse yet, "Will I be alone or lonely?" And why wouldn't women ruminate on these things, when everything from children's toys to adult films to social institutions to various social control mechanisms reinforces these heterogendered messages over and over again?

Given the role of the heterosexual imaginary in concealing the operation of heterosexuality in structuring gender, race, class, and the division of labor, the promise of romance becomes a powerful way to secure women's consent to capitalist patriarchal social arrangements. It represents the promise of a reward—the white wedding—for compliance with the terms of the dominant social order. But it is, after all, illusory. It is a mechanism that secures whiteness as dominant and patriarchal heterosexuality as superior. The promise of a relationship that will provide unconditional love, shore up self-esteem, meet every affective and physical need, and make one feel worthy and fulfilled is compelling. In a high-tech, Internet-permeated, media-based, and alienated commodity culture where goods replace human interaction and shopping anesthetizes us to the realities of life, romance and its pinnacle, the white wedding, become compulsory and necessary for survival. Under these conditions, the white wedding as packaged and sold by the wedding-industrial complex is both homogeneous and the site for the simulation of social relations that we hope will take care of our utopian desires for love, community, belonging, and meaningful labor (Willis 1991).

In addition to constructions of women as feminine subjects in wedding culture, this study has examined the use of gay men and lesbians in the service of heterosexual superiority. During the writing of this book, a young man named Matthew Shepard was murdered in Wyoming simply because he was gay. Reports in the media from interviews with friends and family members of the murderers indicated that they "felt humiliated" that a gay man would "make a pass" at them in front of other people. In fact, they were so humiliated that they found it necessary to beat and torture Shepard and leave him strung to a fence for eighteen hours, after which he eventually died in an area hospital. It was hard to ignore the connection between what I was watching in wedding culture and this "hate crime." As a sociologist, I am trained to inquire into the social conditions that produce various forms of social control, violence being one type. The patterns I observed in the use of gay men and lesbians in wedding culture certainly demonstrate one type of anti-gay violence. The erasure of the humanity of gays and lesbians in the interests of promoting and preserving heterosexual supremacy sends the signal to the viewing public that this "erasure" can be either literal or figurative. Combined with

Gay wedding cake

messages from a variety of other sites, most notably right-wing political conservatives and the religious right, gays and lesbians are uniformly denied their humanity and their dignity and can be seen as expendable or illegitimate in the culture-at-large. Violence takes many forms and exists on a continuum. From the violence of the gay joke to the violence that took a young man's life, they all contribute to the conditions that make anti-gay violence and hate crimes possible.

While wedding culture perpetuates heterosexual supremacy, particularly in relation to its use of gay characters, it also secures white supremacy through its exclusion of historically underrepresented people. More than that, the implied expectation that people of color assimilate to the cultural practices of white America works to both elevate whiteness and perpetuate racial hierarchies. In both instances, the dominant ideologies of difference work to justify and legitimize these practices. When combined with class power, these messages secure the heterosexual imaginary and the privileging of white middle- to upper-class heterosexual marriage over all other forms. The effect of all these social arrangements on the racial and heterogendered division of labor and on the distribution of economic, political, and social resources is profound.

Imagine, if you can, what American culture would be like without romance or the heterosexual imaginary. If we give up the illusions they create or foster, we give up the state of affairs for which we needed illusions.[1] What would take their place? What if we redirected our desires and labor to our real conditions of existence? For example, what if we focused on the creation of a free and democratic society for all, not just for those who represent the dominant interests? The distribution of resources and power would not be based on access to wealth or on who complies with dominant social arrangements. Instead, our relationships, our work, and even our celebrations would transform.

Legal marriage for gay men and lesbians has become a powerful and divisive issue in the late 1990s. Opening access to the institution of marriage, which has as its primary responsibility the distribution of economic power and resources, is very threatening to those who benefit from that power. The state of Hawaii recently passed legislation legalizing marriage for same-sex couples. Challenged in the courts, this legislation will go before the Hawaiian Supreme Court in the next two years. Many experts have argued that it is likely the courts will allow this legislation to stand. As a result, politicians in the federal legislature enacted in 1996 what is now offically called the Defense of Marriage Act. (See Appendix for full text.) According to this new law, no state will be required to honor the legalization of same-sex marriage granted in another state. Given the role of the federal government in the distribution of benefits and social services to married couples, this law also defines, for the first time, what is meant by the word "spouse."

At the same time these issues are being played out on the political front, capi-

Newt Gingrich on weddings and marriage:

On the marriage of his daughter: "I couldn't be happier, or more proud. Every father looks forward to the day when he can look in his daughter's eyes and know that he sees happiness. To a parent, nothing can ever take the place of that moment."

—Holloron 1998

On the marriage of his sister: "I would refuse to attend the wedding. I wouldn't regard it as a marriage. Marriage is between a man and a woman."

—NBC 1996

talists are discovering a new and potentially lucrative market in the lesbian and gay community, a market that would become even more sizable with the legalization of same-sex marriage. Market researchers have targeted this group, and the result has been a proliferation of advertising directed at and making use of gay men and lesbians. IKEA, Banana Republic, Calvin Klein, Absolut Vodka, and most recently AT&T have all contributed to this growing trend. Television programmers have experimented with "the gay kiss" on shows such as ABC's *Roseanne* and *Ellen,* NBC's *Mad About You,* and the recently acclaimed made-for-tv movie, *Serving in Silence: The Margarethe Cammermeyer Story.* Definitions of heterosexuality have been shifting significantly in areas targeted specifically to teenagers and young adults. MTV has had the most impact in this area, since they frequently present shows, videos, and ads providing alternative views of heterosexuality as well as proactive views of gays and lesbians. Critically acclaimed and box office hits such as *The Crying Game, The Wedding Banquet, Love and Death on Long Island,* and *Chasing Amy,* as well as some of those discussed in Chapter 4, have all pressured dominant notions of heterogender and heterosexuality.

Right-wing heterosexual opposition to gay marriage is, in part, grounded in the desire to maintain patriarchal heterosexual supremacy. Those who claim this mantle in the interests of preserving their place of dominance couch their arguments in the rhetoric of morality, as if mere participation in the institution is indicative of moral superiority. Some of the best-kept secrets pertaining to sexuality are held in the name of preserving heterosexuality as the beacon of morality. Obscured from view is the reality that many acts of violence are committed from within the institution of patriarchal heterosexuality: domestic violence, child sexual abuse (over 90 percent of the cases are adult male to female child), marital rape, sexual harrassment, and pornography, to name a few. Along with the hysterical fantasies about the consequences of gay and lesbian marriages, remarks abound equating legal marriage for gays and lesbians with morality out of control and polygamy as the ultimate objective.

In reality, patriarchal monogamous heterosexuality is in crisis, and the petitioning of homosexuals for equal standing under the law is bringing this crisis to light. Claims of adultery are symptoms of real conditions of existence that reveal the level of informal polygamy rampant in patriarchal cultures. Research suggests that the degree to which men and women experience affective and sexual relations outside the institution of marriage is more normative than deviant.

Within the gay community, the marriage debates have taken on significant momentum as gays and lesbians seek normalization and access to a wide array of rewards and benefits. (See Appendix for listing.) The pro-marriage advocates argue that access to marriage will go a long way toward mainstreaming gay and lesbian relationships. They believe that participation in marriage would open up other possibilities: reduction in hate crimes and employment discrimination and fewer court battles over child custody. The pro side is very compelling as it relates to material resources, but it still leaves open the exclusion of these same benefits for people who are not coupled—or not traditionally coupled—regardless of sexuality.

On the anti-marriage side from within the gay/lesbian community, the argument is against assimilation into a culture not of their own making, a culture that has historically served as the gatekeeper for power. To participate in the institution of marriage as it is currently organized is to legitimize the institution of heterosexuality and the heterosexual imaginary, virtually all the practices outlined in this study. This argument is equaling compelling given the racial, gender, and class interests preserved and perpetuated through the institution of marriage.

Critical heterosexual studies is not a new idea but is rapidly developing into a new field of study. Nineteenth-century marriage reform activists were very active in challenging church and state control over heterosexual relations, and twentieth-century feminists Adrienne Rich, Charlotte Bunch, Monique Wittig, Rita Mae Brown, and others offered groundbreaking critiques of heterosexuality as compulsory and as an institution. Within the social sciences, research on marriage and family abounds and has had a significant impact on our understandings of these institutions and on policy-making. As sizable as this body of work is, few studies have focused critically on the relationship of marriage and family to the institution of heterosexuality. Important critiques have recently emerged in lesbian/gay/transgendered studies, cultural studies, psychology, sociology, and history. Among these recent works, Jonathan Katz's history of heterosexuality, *The Invention of Heterosexuality* (1996) is a major contribution. *Theorising Heterosexuality* (1996), edited by Diane Richardson, provides contributions from notable theorists including Stevi Jackson, Jo Van Every, Sheila Jeffreys, Caroline Ramazanoglu, and Carol Smart. And *(Hetero)sexual Politics* (1995), edited by Mary Maynard and June Purvis, offers a collection of works by some of the same authors, relecting contemporary debates on the politics of heterosexuality.

This study, *White Weddings: Romancing Heterosexuality in Popular Culture*, provides one of the first studies of weddings in the United States and serves as another example of critical heterosexual studies. It has been my hope that this book would provide an opening for many others to take the field of critical heterosexual studies further into subjects such as heterosexuality and the law, heterosexuality and labor, heterosexuality and medicine, the tyranny of coupling, marriage resistance, and other dominant heterosexual practices and rituals including critiques of the marriage and family research and textbooks. Beyond this, there are numerous books to be written dealing with the ubiquitous wedding, including interview studies with brides about the meaning-making processes involved in the wedding, the experience of purchasing the bridal gown, and what it means to take someone else's name. There are many, many options available for expanding this area. Here comes the bride!

Epilogue

They seated the married people together. It was a wedding reception at a traditional white wedding in the 1980s. I was a guest, an unmarried guest. When it came time for me to be seated I was placed at a table on the far edge of the dining area, far away from my married friends, with people who were either divorced, widowed, single, or gay, or, as the "wedding singer" proclaimed, "the table of mutants." Combined with all the times I'd been asked, "So, when is it *your* turn?" or "We seated you with all the single, eligible men! Isn't that great?" this episode was just one among many I had endured over the years. I knew I wasn't alone in this experience and was always amazed at how few people complained.

Writing this book has been a wrenching experience. Without realizing how fully I've been sutured to dominant heterosexual culture, I have frequently found myself engaged in a variety of internal struggles. Watching video after video of wedding stories, there were times when I would feel my emotions and my intellect split apart. Tears would be streaming down my face as I empathized with the characters in a movie while, at the same time, I would be taking notes critiquing the heterosexual imaginary. It was this "splitting apart" that revealed to me the depth and reach of cultural forces in securing our compliance and the strength of conviction needed to counter or resist these forces. What this told me, in ways I hadn't realized to this extent, was how difficult it really is to become antiracist, antiheterosexist, anticlassist, anti-anything oppressive. It requires developing the ability to do the critique, envisioning resistance, enlisting creativity, and making change happen while simultaneously hearing the voices and feeling the feelings associated with the dominant. It is the experience of splitting the self: the racialized, heterogendered, class-based, sexualized conscious and unconscious. The implications for undertaking critical studies of dominance are profound. They reveal the depth of the indoctrination and the considerable effort required for making social change.

Considering the ways the heterosexual imaginary conceals our real conditions of existence, I also did not realize the degree to which this would be true. Even the lessons I learned in doing this study did not prepare me for what I witnessed recently in the free trade zones along the U.S./Mexican border. I traveled with a delegation sponsored by the New York State Labor and Religion Coalition to Valle Hermosa and Matamoros, Mexico, to meet with workers laboring in maquiladoras there. What we witnessed gave significantly more urgency to what is revealed in these pages. American and other foreign corporations such as Fruit of the Loom, General Motors, Ford, Chrysler, and Wal-Mart, as well as many smaller companies, are making use of NAFTA to cut costs and increase profits at the expense of the people, lands, culture, and children in this region. As witnesses to atrocities being committed in the name of "good business" and free trade, we saw thousands of working people and their families forced to live on top of landfills and toxic waste dumps, in one room shanties with little or no water. The workers toil more than eight hours every day, with no restrictions on how much mandatory overtime they are forced to work, no child care, little or no protections from workplace hazards and for an average salary of $19 per week.[1] We heard stories of women forced to bring used sanitary napkins to work to prove they were not pregnant, of employers who regularly distributed birth control pills, of varying degrees of sexual harassment and abuse. We met families where their children had died of massive birth defects and disease from exposure to toxins in the environment and in the workplace. And we met workers whose health had been so severely compromised that many were unable to work anymore as a result of disabling conditions such as carpal tunnel syndrome and cancers. What was most extraordinary about this trip was the dignity, conviction, and commitment to community and life these people displayed. Under the most severe living conditions imaginable they welcomed us into their homes and their hearts, even in the face of the undeniable realization that our comfort, our privilege, our booming economy in the U.S. depends upon these conditions.

Activists such as Martha Ojeda, Manuel Mondragon, and Jaime Salinas of the Coalition for Justice in the Maquiladoras are among the many around the world working to save the lives of their people. For them, there is no romance, only the love that comes with working every day to deal with their real conditions of existence.

What allows us to imagine possibilities? To continue to live shrouded in romance is to participate in and benefit from such atrocities. Confronting the reasons for which we need romance is to see what it conceals. Critiquing the heterosexual imaginary is one step in that direction.

Bride and maid of
honor, 1971

Appendix

The Comstock Act: 18 U.S. Code, Section 1461

1461. *Mailing obscene or crime-inciting matter.* Every obscene, lewd, lascivious, indecent, filthy or vile article, matter, thing, device or substance; and—

Every article or thing designed, adapted, or intended for preventing conception or producing abortion, or for any indecent or immoral use; and

Every article, instrument, substance, drug, medicine, or thing which is advertised or described in a manner calculated to lead another to use or apply it for preventing conception or producing abortion, or for any indecent or immoral purpose; and

Every written or printed card, letter, circular, book pamphlet, advertisement, or notice of any kind giving information, directly or indirectly, where, or how, or from whom, or by what means any of such mentioned matters, articles, or things may be obtained or made, or where or by whom any act or operation of any kind for the procuring or producing of abortion will be done or performed, or how or by what means conception may be prevented or abortion produced, whether sealed or unsealed; and

Every paper, writing, advertisement, or representation that any article, instrument, substance, drug, medicine, or thing may, or can, be used or applied for preventing conception or producing abortion, or for any indecent or immoral purpose; and

Every description calculated to induce or incite a person to so use or apply any such article, instrument, substance, drug, medicine, or thing—

Is declared to be nonmailable matter and shall not be conveyed in the mails or delivered from any post office or by any letter carrier.

Whoever knowingly uses the mails for the mailing, carriage in the mails, or delivery of anything declared by this section to be nonmailable, or knowingly causes to be delivered by mail according to the direction thereon, or at the place at which it is directed to be delivered by the person to whom it is addressed, or knowingly takes any such thing from the mails for the purpose of circulating or disposing thereof, or of aiding in the circulation or disposition thereof, shall be fined not more than $5,000 or imprisoned not more than five years, or both, for the first such offense, and shall be fined not more than $10,000 or imprisoned not more than ten years, or both, for each such offense thereafter.

The term "indecent," as used in this section includes matter of a character tending to incite arson, murder, or assassination.

The Defense of Marriage Act (1996)

To define and protect the institution of marriage. <<Note: Sept. 21, 1996–[H.R. 3396]>>

Be it enacted by the Senate and House of Representatives of the United States of America in Congress assembled, <<Note: Defense of Marriage Act.>>

Section 1. <<Note: 1 USC 1 note.>> Short Title.

This Act may be cited as the "Defense of Marriage Act."

Sec. 2. Powers Reserved to the States.
   (a.) In General—Chapter 115 of title 28, United States Code, is amended by adding after section 1738B the following:
   "Sec. 1738C. Certain acts, records, and proceedings and the effect thereof
   "No State, territory, or possession of the United States, or Indian tribe, shall be required to give effect to any public act, record, or judicial proceeding of any other State, territory, possession, or tribe respecting a relationship between persons of the same sex that is treated as a marriage under the laws of such other State, territory, possession, or tribe, or a right or claim arising from such relationship."
   (b.) Clerical Amendment.—The table of sections at the beginning of chapter 115 of title

28, United States Code, is amended by inserting after the item relating to section 1738B the following new item:

"1738C. Certain acts, records, and proceedings and the effect thereof."

Sec. 3. Definition of Marriage.

(a) In General.—Chapter 1 of title 1, United States Code, is amended by adding at the end of the following:

"Sec. 7. Definition of "marriage" and "spouse.""

"In determining the meaning of any Act of Congress, or of any ruling, regulation, or interpretation of the various administrative bureaus and agencies of the United States, the word "marriage" means only a legal union between one man and one woman as husband and wife, and the word "spouse" refers only to a person of the opposite sex who is a husband or a wife."

Public Law 104–199
104th Congress
July 11, 12, 1996, considered and passed House.
Sept. 10, considered and passed Senate.

State-Granted Legal Marriage Rights

Assumption of Spouse's Pension
Automatic Inheritance
Automatic Housing Lease Transfer
Bereavement Leave
Burial Determination
Child Custody
Crime Victim's Recovery Benefits
Divorce Protections
Domestic Violence Protection
Exemption from Property Tax on Partner's Death
Immunity from Testifying Against Spouse
Insurance Breaks

Joint Adoption and Foster Care
Joint Automobile Insurance
Joint Bankruptcy
Joint Parenting (Insurance Coverage, School Records)
Medical Decisions on Behalf of Partner
Medical Insurance Family Coverage
Certain Property Rights
Reduced-Rate Memberships
Sick Leave to Care for Partner
Visitation of Partner's Children
Visitation of Partner in Hospital or Prison
Wrongful Death (Loss of Consort) Benefits

Federally Granted Legal Marriage Rights

Access to Military Stores
Assumption of Spouse's Pension
Bereavement Leave
Immigration
Insurance Breaks
Medical Decisions on Behalf of Partner
Sick Leave to Care for Partner
Tax Breaks
Veteran's Discounts
Visitation of Partner in Hospital or Prison

Source: Partners Task Force for Gay & Lesbian Couples, 1998

Wedding Movies
from 1890-1999

Wedding (1990)

Wedding, A (1978)

The Wedding (1986)

Wedding Band (1998)

Wedding Bell Blues (1996)

Wedding Belle (1947)

Wedding Bells (1933)

Wedding Bells (1921)

Wedding Belts (1940)

Wedding Blues (1920)

Wedding Gown, The (1913)

Wedding Group (1936)

Wedding in Monaco, The (1956)

Wedding in White (1972)

Wedding Knight, A (1966)

Wedding March, The (1928)

Wedding Night, The (1935)

Wedding Night Blues (1995)

Wedding Nights (1976)

The Wedding of Jack and Jill (1930)

The Wedding of Lilli Marlene (1953)

A Wedding on Walton's Mountain (1982)

The Wedding Party (1969)

The Wedding Present (1936)

Wedding Rehearsal (1932)

Wedding Rings (1930)

Wedding Rituals (1995)

The Wedding Singer (1998)

The Wedding Song (1925)

The Wedding Tape (1996)

The Wedding That Didn't Come Off (1910)

Wedding Vows (1994)

The Wedding Was Beautiful . . . . (1972)

Wedding Women (1924)

Wedding Worries (1941)

Wedding and Babies (1958)

Weddings are Wonderful (1939)

Her Wedding Night (1930)

Her Wedding Night (1911)

His Wedding Night (1917)

His Wedding Scare (1943)

Four Weddings and a Funeral (1994)

Joe's Wedding (1996)

The Fatal Wedding (1911)

Lili's Wedding Night (1952)

Quiet Wedding (1940)

His Wedding Night (1917)

Four Weddings and a Honeymoon (1955) (V)

Joe's Wedding (1996)

Fatal Wedding, The (1911)

Quiet Wedding (1940)

Royal Wedding (1951)

. . . aka *Wedding Bells* (1951)

Swing Wedding (1937)

White Wedding (1995) (V)

White Wedding (1994) (V)

Betsy's Wedding (1990)

Double Wedding (1937)

Double Wedding (1933)

Double Wedding, A (1913)

Fanny's Wedding Day (1933)

Golden Wedding, The (1913)

On Her Wedding Night (1915)

On His Wedding Day (1913)

Polish Wedding (1998)

Public Wedding (1937)

Silver Wedding (1974) (TV)

Walton Wedding, A (1995) (TV)

Coster's Wedding, The (1910)

Muriel's Wedding (1994)

Shotgun Wedding (1963)

Shotgun Wedding (1993)

Tricia's Wedding (1972)

Waikiki Wedding (1937)

Barbara's Wedding (1973) (TV)

Diabolic Wedding (1971)

. . . aka *Diabolique Wedding* (1971)

Gasoline Wedding, A (1918)

Midnight Wedding, The (1912)

Rebecca's Wedding Day (1914)

Emergency Wedding (1950)

Chuppa: The Wedding Canopy (1994)

His Wooden Wedding (1925)

Wooing and Wedding of a Coon, The (1905)

Dr. Kildare's Wedding Day (1941)

. . . aka *Mary Names the Day* (1941)

Her Strange Wedding (1917)

My Brother's Wedding (1984)

Pastry Town Wedding (1934)

Undertaker's Wedding, The (1997)

Her Dog-Gone Wedding (1920)

Quiet Little Wedding, A (1920)

Satan's Black Wedding (1975)

Their Golden Wedding (1915)

Member of the Wedding, The (1952)

Member of the Wedding, The (1997) (TV)

Pauline Calf's Wedding Video (1994) (TV)

. . . aka *Three Fights, Two Weddings and a*

Funeral (1994) (TV)

Circle C Ranch Wedding Present (1910)

Clancy's Kosher Wedding (1927)

Johnson at the Wedding (1911)

My Girlfriend's Wedding (1969)

Eight Is Enough Wedding, An (1989) (TV)

My Best Friend's Wedding (1997)

Two Wives at One Wedding (1960)

Invitation to the Wedding (1985)

Saved by the Bell: Wedding in Las Vegas (1994) (TV)

Three Thieves and a Wedding (1991)

La Cage aux Folles 3: The Wedding (1985)

Some matches were also found among the alternative titles (akas)

Hsi Yen (1993)

. . . aka *Wedding Banquet, The* (1993)

Gong zi jiao (1981)

. . . aka *Wedding Bells, Wedding Belles* (1981)

Catered Affair, The (1956)

. . . aka *Wedding Breakfast* (1956)

Going to the Chapel (1988) (TV)

. . . aka *Wedding Day* (1988) (TV)

Baishey Shravana (1960)

. . . aka *Wedding Day, The* (1960/I)

Brollopsdagen (1960)

. . . aka *Wedding Day, The* (1960/II)

Mangryongui Wechingturesu (1980)

. . . *Wedding Dress of the Ghost* (1980)

Svadebny podarok (1982)

. . .aka *Wedding Gift* (1982)

Wide-Eyed and Legless (1994) (TV)

. . . aka *Wedding Gift, The* (1994) (TV)

Obvinyayetsya svadba (1986)

. . . *Wedding Is Accused, The* (1986)

Naszindulo (1943)

. . . aka *Wedding March* (1943)

Kekkon koshinkyoku (1951)

. . . aka *Wedding March* (1951)

Vasil Ni Raat (1929)

. . . aka *Wedding Night* (1929)

Hochzaeitsnuecht (1992)

. . . aka *Wedding Night—End of the Song* (1992)

Bryllupsnatten (1997)

. . . aka *Wedding Night, The* (1997)

Turkischen Gurken, Die (1962)

. . . aka *Wedding Present* (1962)

Kyurun Iyagi (1993)

. . . aka *Wedding Story* (1993)

Vase de noces (1974)

. . . aka *Wedding Trough* (1974)

Noces rouges, Les (1973)

. . . aka *Wedding in Blood* (1973)

Urs al-jalil (1987)

. . . aka *Wedding in Galilee* (1987)

Svadba v Malinovke (1967)

. . . aka *Wedding in Malinovka* (1967)

Hochzeit im Excentricclub, Die (1917)

. . . aka *Wedding in the Eccentric Club* (1917)

Kajak (1933)

. . . aka *Wedding of Palo, The* (1937)

Wesela nie bedzie (1978)

. . . aka *Wedding's Off* (1978)

Svadba (1944)

. . . aka *Wedding, The* (1944)

Wesele (1972)

. . . aka *Wedding, The* (1972)

Dugun—Die Heirat (1992)

. . . aka *Wedding, The* (1992)

Leprechaun 2 (1994)

. . . aka *One Wedding and a Lot of Funerals* (1994)

Kivenpyorittajan kyla (1995)

. . . aka *Last Wedding, The* (1995)

He Knows You're Alone (1980)

. . . aka *Blood Wedding* (1980)

Boadas de Sangre (1981)

. . . aka *Blood Wedding* (1981)

Noces de papier, Les (1989) (TV)

. . . aka *Paper Wedding, A* (1989) (TV)

Nunta de piatra (1972)

. . . aka *Stone Wedding* (1972)

Noce blanche (1989)

. . . aka *White Wedding* (1989)

Hang choh yan yuen lo (1984)

. . . aka *Wrong Wedding Trail* (1984)

Medvezh'ya svad'ba (1926)

. . . aka *Bear's Wedding, The* (1926)

Boda secreta (1988)

. . . aka *Secret Wedding* (1989)

Plenilunio delle vergini, Il (1973)

. . . aka *Devil's Wedding Night, The* (1973) (USA)

Sita Kalyanam (1976)

. . . aka *Seeta's Wedding* (1976)

Brollopsbesvar (1964)

. . . aka *Swedish Wedding Night* (1964)

Jia qinao fan tian (ND)

. . . aka *Undated Wedding* (ND)

Nozze vagabonde (1936)

. . . aka *Beggar's Wedding* (1936)

Hochzeit von Lanneken, Die (1964)
. . . aka *Lanneken Wedding, The* (1964)
Povtornaya svadba (1975)
. . . aka *Repeated Wedding* (1975)
Lebassi Baraye Arossi (1976)
. . . aka *Suit for Wedding, A* (1976)
Rubezahls Hochzeit (1916)
. . . aka *Old Nip's Wedding* (1916)
Don Juan heiratet (1909)
. . . aka *Don Juan's Wedding* (1909)
Parvathi Kalyanam (1936)
. . . aka *Parvathi's Wedding* (1936)
Million v brachnoy korzine (1986)
. . . aka *Million in a Wedding Basket* (1986)
Kogda opazdyvayut v ZAGS . . . (1991)
. . . aka *When You're Late For Wedding . . .*
   (1991)
Skaz pro to, kak tsar Pyotr arapa zhenil
   (1976)
. . . aka *Tale About Czar Pyotr Arranging*
   Arap's Wedding (1976)

Bride Movies
Bride, The (1929)
Bride, The (1987)
Bride, The (1985/I)
Bride 13 (1920)
Bride and Gloom (1918)
Bride and Gloom (1954)
Bride and Gloom (1921)
Bride and the Beast, The (1958)
. . . aka *Queen of the Gorillas* (1958)
Bride by Mistake (1944)
Bride Came C.O.D., The (1941)

Bride Comes Home, The (1935)
Bride For a Knight, A (1923)
Bride for Henry, A (1937)
Bride for Sale (1949)
Bride Goes Wild, The (1948)
Bride in Black, The (1990) (TV)
Bride of Boogedy (1987) (TV)
Bride of Chucky (1998)
. . . aka *Child's Play 4* (1998) (working title)
. . . aka *Child's Play 4: Bride of Chucky*
   (1998) (working title)
Bride of Fear, The (1918)
Bride of Frankenstein (1935)
. . . aka *Frankenstein Lives Again!* (1935)
   (USA: working title)
. . . aka *Return of Frankenstein, The* (1935)
   (USA: working title)
Bride of Killer Nerd (1992)
Bride of Lammermoor, The (1909)
Bride of Re-Animator (1990)
. . . aka *Re-Animator 2* (1990)
Bride of the Andes (1966)
Bride of the Colorado, The (1928)
Bride of the Desert (1929)
Bride of the Gorilla (1951)
Bride of the Head of the Family (1998)
Bride of the Incredible Hulk (1979) (TV)
Bride of the Lake, The (1934)
. . . aka *Lily of Killarney* (1934)
Bride of the Monster (1955)
. . . aka *Bride of the Atom* (1955)
. . . aka *Monster of the Marshes* (1955) (work-
   ing title)
Bride of the Regiment (1930)

...aka *Lady of the Rose* (1930)

Bride of the Storm (1926)

Bride of Vengeance (1949)

Bride Stripped Bare, The (1967)

Bride Stripped Bare (1994) (V)

Bride sur le cou, La (1961)

...aka *Only For Love* (1961)

..aka *Please Not Now!* (1963)

Bride To Be (1974)

Bride Walks Out, The (1936)

Bride Wore Boots, The (1946)

Bride Wore Crutches, The (1940)

Bride Wore Red, The (1937)

Bridegrooms Beware (1913)

Brideless Groom (1947)

Brides Are Like That (1936)

Bride's Awakening, The (1918)

Bride's Bereavement, The (1932)

...aka *Snake in the Grass* (1932)

Bride's Confession, The (1922)

Brides of Blood (1968)

...aka *Brides of Blood Island* (1968)

...aka *Brides of Death* (1968)

...aka *Brides of the Beast* (1968)

...aka *Grave Desires* (1979/I) (reissue title)

...aka *Island of the Living Horror* (1968)

...aka *Orgy of Blood* (1968)

...aka *Terror on Blood Island* (1968)

Brides of Dracula, The (1960)

Brides of Fu Manchu, The (1966)

Brides of Sulu (1934)

Bride's Play (1922)

Bride's Relations, The (1929)

Bride's Silence, The (1917)

Brides Wore Blood, The (1972)

...aka *Blood Bride* (1972)

Bridesmaids (1989) (TV)

Mr. Bride (1932)

Bad Bride, The (1985)

Gay Bride, The (1934)

...aka *Repeal* (1934) (working title)

One Bride Too Many (ND)

Sky Bride (1932)

Two Brides (1919)

War Bride (1928)

War Brides (1916)

War Brides (1980) (TV)

War Bride's Secret, The (1916)

Demi-Bride, The (1927)

Fire Bride, The (1922)

Fly's Bride, The (1929)

June Bride (1998)

June Bride, The (1926)

June Bride, A (1935)

June Bride (1948)

Lost Bridegroom, The (1916)

...aka *His Lost Self* (1916)

Mail Bride, A (1932)

Snow Bride, The (1923)

Some Bride (1919)

Arab's Bride, The (1912)

Blood Bride (1980)

...aka *Death of a Nun* (1980)

Child Bride (1938)

...aka *Child Bride of the Ozarks* (1938)

Child Bride of Short Creek (1981) (TV)

Elven Bride, The (1995) (V)

Muddy Bride, A (1921)

Night Bride (1927)

Seven Brides for Seven Brothers (1954)

Young Bride (1932)

. . . aka *Love Starved* (1932)

Beggar Bride, The (1997) (TV)

Bingo, Bridesmaids & Braces (1976)

Bronze Bride, The (1917)

Chased Bride, The (1923)

Corpse Bride, The (ND)

Desert Bride, The (1928)

Desert Bridegroom, The (1922)

Forged Bride, The (1920)

G.I. War Brides (1946)

Half a Bride (1928)

Jungle Bride (1933)

Little Bride of Heaven, The (1912)

Masked Bride, The (1925)

Secret Bride, The (1935)

. . . aka *Concealment* (1935)

Stolen Bride, The (1927)

Stolen Bride, The (1913)

Zandy's Bride (1974)

. . . aka *For Better, For Worse* (1974)

30 Foot Bride of Candy Rock, The (1959)

. . . aka *Lou Costello and His 30 Foot Bride* (1959)

. . . aka *Secret Bride of Candy Rock, The* (1959)

Lottery Bride, The (1930)

Missing Bride, A (1914)

Missing Bridegroom, The (1910)

Nobody's Bride (1923)

Outlaw's Bride, The (1915)

Perfect Bride, The (1991) (TV)

Picture Bride (1995)

Picture Brides (1933)

Pullman Bride, A (1917)

Ranger's Bride, The (1910)

Runaway Bride (1999)

Runaway Bride, The (1930)

Scarlet Bride (1989)

Spectre Bridegroom, The (1913)

Teenage Bride (1970)

Always a Bride (1953)

Always a Bride (1940)

Always a Bridesmaid (1943)

Bachelor Brides (1926)

Backdoor Brides 3 (1988) (V)

Backdoor Brides 4 (1993) (V)

Bartered Bride, The (1913)

Blushing Bride, The (1921)

Broadway Bride, The (1921)

December Bride (1990)

Fireman's Bride, The (1931)

His Jazz Bride (1926)

Imported Bridegroom, The (1990)

Kiss the Bride Goodbye (1944)

Leopard's Bride, The (1916)

Midnight Bride, The (1920)

Old Man's Bride, The (1967)

. . . aka *Bride, The* (1967)

Princess Bride, The (1987)

Prodigal Bridegroom, A (1926)

Roping a Bride (1915)

She-Male Bride Exposed (1992) (V)

Too Many Brides (1914)

. . . aka *Love Chase, The* (1914)

Unkissed Bride, The (1966)

. . . aka *Mother Goose a Go-Go* (1966)

All for a Bride (1927)

Cave Man's Bride, The (1919)

Love That Bride (1950)

Perplexed Bridegroom, The (1914)

Reluctant Bride (1955)

Delinquent Bridegroom, The (1916)

Frightened Bride, The (1953)

. . . aka *Tall Headlines, The* (1953)

Mail Order Bride (1984)

Mail Order Bride, The (1912)

Mail Order Bride (1964)

. . . aka *West of Montana* (1964)

Rebellious Bride, The (1919)

Ride for a Bride (1913)

Rustling a Bride (1919)

Song for a Bride (1958)

Baby of the Bride (1991) (TV)

Seventeenth Bride, The (1986)

Unfortunate Bride, The (1932)

. . . aka *Ungluckliche Kale, Die* (1932) (Yiddish title: alternative title)

Dangers of a Bride (1917)

Happy Is the Bride (1957)

Japanese War Bride (1952)

Our Blushing Brides (1930)

Price of the Bride, The (1990) (TV)

Professional Bride (1941)

Well-Groomed Bride, The (1946)

Beware of the Bride (1920)

Father of the Bride (1991)

Father of the Bride (1950)

Father of the Bride Part II (1995)

Honeymoon: The Bride's Running Behind, The (1990)

Mother of the Bride (1993) (TV)

Slave for the Bride, A (1991) (V)

Troubles of a Bride (1925)

Here Comes the Bride (1919)

Here Comes the Bride (1981)

Here Comes the Bridesmaid (1928)

There Goes the Bride (1979)

There Goes the Bride (1932)

Children of the Bride (1990) (TV)

Making of Seven Brides for Seven Brothers, The (1997) (TV)

I Was a Male War Bride (1949)

. . . aka *You Can't Sleep Here* (1949)

Two Grooms for a Bride (1957)

Bulldog Drummond's Bride (1939)

. . . aka *Mr. and Mrs. Bulldog Drummond* (1939) (USA: working title)

I Was a Mail Order Bride (1982) (TV)

Case of the Curious Bride, The (1935)

Night of the Devil's Bride (1975)

They All Kissed the Bride (1942)

World's Oldest Living Bridesmaid, The (1990) (TV)

Black Daisies for the Bride (1993) (TV)

Diary of a High School Bride (1959)

Vendetta: Secrets of a Mafia Bride (1991) (TV)

. . . aka *Bride of Violence* (1991) (TV)

. . . aka *Donna d'onore* (1991) (TV)

. . . aka *Family Matter, A* (1991) (TV)

King's Quest VII: The Princeless Bride (1994)

Family Video Diaries: Daughter of the Bride (1997) (TV)

Perry Mason: The Case of the Heartbroken Bride (1992) (TV)

Endnotes

Chapter 1

1. Unfortunately, the only source for data on the wedding industry is produced by the industry itself. More objective studies of wedding industry statistics need to be conducted.
2. This booklet was probably co-authored by his wife, Angela, but her name was kept out of the publication for fear Comstock would arrest her as well. In addition to having children who needed attending, prison conditions were thought of as particularly deplorable for respectable, middle-class, white women.
3. The official record refers to this as the Markland letter.
4. As part of the "General Education" requirement for entering students at Russell Sage College for women, first-year students are expected to complete a course called "Women in the World." The texts for this course are six biographical works on such notables as Rosalind Franklin, posthumously awarded the Nobel Prize in science for her work on DNA, and Rigoberta Menchu, Nobel Peace Prize winner from Guatemala. Frequently, students at the beginning of the semester comment that they feared this course because of its "male-bashing" and "femi-nazi" content. By the end of the semester they realize that nothing of the sort has occurred.
5. I want to thank Rosemary Hennessy for her valuable assistance in theorizing this concept.
6. See Bunch 1975; Harman 1901; Heywood 1876; MacDonald 1972; Sears 1977; Stoehr 1979; Wittig 1975.

7. "'Relations of ruling' is a concept that grasps power, organization, direction, and regulation as more pervasively structured than can be expressed in traditional concepts provided by the discourses of power. I have come to see a specific interrelation between the dynamic advance of the distinctive forms of organizing and ruling contemporary capitalist society and the patriarchal forms of our contemporary experience" (Smith 1987, 3).

8. "Heterogender is the asymmetrical stratification of the sexes in relation to the historically varying institutions of patriarchal heterosexuality. This concept demystifies the linkage of gender as an organizing concept for heterosexuality" (Ingraham 1994).

Chapter 2

1. For an illuminating exposé of today's white weddings, see the excellent article "Something Old, Something New," in the March/April 1997 issue of *Might* magazine.

2. The language we use for identifying the race and ethnicity of people is frequently very awkward. To identify a group by color helps to perpetuate notions of race and racialization; to identify in terms of ethnicity erases the experience and effects of racism or of racial hierarchies. Much of the data presented here come from official sources. Almost without exception those sources use white, black, or hispanic as identifying categories. To be consistent with these sources I've use the racialized categories, though I am not comfortable with this option and generally believe we should rely on cultural signifiers such as African, Latino, or Native American, for example. However, even this type of identification is problematic given that many of us do not belong exclusively to one category. As for hispanic, the debates over identification with the Spanish colonialists or with Latino history is a source of great debate. In this case, I've used hispanic instead of Latino primarily because of the earlier explanation. However, I have put it in lower case as a way to diminish its weight in relation to an imperialist history.

3. Not included in these figures but related to the wedding industry is the current boom in fiftieth wedding anniversary celebrations, which frequently include many of the same arrangements and expense. While later generations divorced more frequently, parents of baby boomers stayed married, and many of them are now celebrating this milestone in heterosexual culture.

   Additionally, the wedding industry has identified another lucrative niche in the lesbian and gay marriage market. As lesbians and gays await the final ruling by the Hawaiian Supreme Court on the legalization of gay marriage, a variety of businesses, especially the travel industry, are poised to serve this previously untapped market.

4. Black women are 5.5 times more likely to be receiving Aid to Families with Dependent Children than white women (20 percent versus 3.5 percent) (Besharov and Sullivan 1996).

5. Domestic relations laws citation.

6. Ibid.

7. NAFTA is the acronym for the North Atlantic Free Trade Agreement signed by President Clinton in 1992. It took effect on January 1, 1994.

8. GATT is the acronym for the General Agreement on Tariffs and Trade.

9. The laws pertaining to marriage use the term "Indian" and "white" and have not been updated since 1888.

10. Targets of the Disney boycott are Disney's theme parks; Disney stores; Walt Disney Pictures, Touchstone, Miramax, Hollywood, and Caravan Picture; ABC television and radio networks; individual shows including *Home Improvement, Ellen, Live! With Regis and Kathie Lee*, and *Siskel & Ebert*; the Disney Channel; ESPN; A&E television network; Lifetime; Mighty Ducks of Anaheim, National Hockey League franchise; Anaheim Angels, American League baseball team; Hollywood Records; *Discover* magazine; and several Disney plays such as "Lion King" and "Beauty and the Beast."

Chapter 4

1. The reference to illusion in this analysis comes from a passage by Karl Marx in the introduction to *Contribution to the Critique of Hegel's Philosophy of Law* (1844). With the elegance of a poet, Marx argues that religion is the "sigh of an oppressed people," who need the illusion of well-being rather than confront the source of their oppression and create "real" happiness. "To abolish religion as the illusory happiness of the people is to demand their real happiness. The demand to give up illusions about the existing state of affairs is the demand to give up a state of affairs which needs illusions. The criticism of religion is therefore in embryo the criticism of the vale of tears, the halo of which is religion. Criticism has torn up the imaginary flowers from the chain not so that man shall wear the unadorned, bleak chain but so that he will shake off the chain and pluck the living flower." This metaphor applies to all those sites that we use to numb us to the our real conditions of existence. One could substitute the word romance for religion and the meaning of this passage would still hold.

Chapter 5

1. Paraphrased from Karl Marx, *Contribution to the Critique of Hegel's Philosophy of Law,* 1844.

Epilogue

1. This figure varies to some degree from source to source but never exceeds $37 per week.

References

Ackerman, D. 1994. *A natural history of love.* New York: Random House.

Agger, Ben. 1992. *Cultural studies as critical theory.* London: Falmer.

Albany Times Union. 1998. People in the news: Dreams come true for actress's movie concept. (October 11): A2.

Althusser, Louis. 1976. *Essays in self-criticism.* Atlantic Highlands, NJ: Humanities Press.

———. 1971. *Lenin and philosophy and other essay,* translated by Ben Brewster. New York: Monthly Review.

———. 1970. *For marx,* translated by Ben Brewster. London: NLB.

Althusser, Louis, and Etienne Balibar. 1968. *Reading capital,* translated by Ben Brewster. London: NLB.

American Gem Society. 1998. *The power of love.* www.org/info/lovetour

Anderson, Susan Heller. 1981. The dress: Silk taffeta with sequins and pearls. *New York Times* (July 30); A2.

Anner, John. 1996. Sweatshop workers organize and win. *The Progressive* (June).

Atkinson, Dan. 1998. Diamonds get facet lift. *Guardian.* PSA–2047.

Bedrick, Barry. 1997. U.S. General Accounting Office: On the effects of DOMA. Partners Task Force for Gay & Lesbian Couples. (January 31). www.buddybuddy.com/marfeda.html

Bennett, Claudette. 1995. *The black population in the US: March 1994 and 1993.* Washington, DC: US Department of Commerce Economics and Statistics Administration and the Census Bureau.

Bernard, Joan Kelly. 1995. Calling it off when pre-wedding jitters are more than that. *Newsday* (June 27): p. B17.

Bernardo, F.M. and H. Vera. 1981. The groomal shower. A variation of the American bridal shower. *Family relations, 30, 395–401.*

Besharov, Douglas J. and Timothy Sullivan. 1996. Welfare reform and marriage. *The Public Interest* (September 1); 14, 81.

Black, Robert W. 1998. Family of gay man thank public. *Yahoo! News* (October 16); http://dailynews.yahoo.com/headlines/ap

Blatt, Martin. 1989. *Free love and anarchism.* Chicago: University of Chicago Press.

Boswell, John. 1994. *Same-sex unions in premodern Europe.* New York: Villard Books.

Bourdieu, Pierre. 1984. *Distinction: A social critique of the judgement of taste.* Translated by Richard Nice. Cambridge, MA: Harvard University Press.

Brewer, Rose. 1997. Theorizing race, class, and gender: The new scholarship of Black feminist intellectuals and Black women's labor. In *Materialist Feminism: A Reader in Class, Difference and Women's Lives.* New York: Routledge.

Bride's. 1998. Train of thought. *Bride's* (August/September): p. 6.

———. 1997/1998. Princess bride. *Bride's* (December/January): 40.

———. 1997a. *Bride's American marriage today: facts & figures.* New York: Conde Naste.

———. 1997b. *Bride's millenium report: Love & money.* New York: Conde Naste.

———. 1995/1996. *Bridal market acquisition report.* New York: Conde Naste.

Brown, Rita Mae. 1976. *Plain brown rapper.* Baltimore: Diana Press.

Bunch, Charlotte. 1995. *Paying the price: Women and the politics of international economic strategy.* London: Zed.

———. 1994. *Demanding accountability: The global campaign and Vienna tribunal for women's human rights.* New Brunswick, NJ: Rutgers University Press.

———. 1987. *Passionate politics: Feminist theory in action.* New York: St. Martin's Press.

———. 1975. Not for lesbians only. *Quest: A Feminist Quarterly.* (Fall).

Cacas, Samuel. 1994. Clothing designer tries a court order to stifle protests over seamstresses. *AsianWeek* (August 5).

Callinicos, Alex. 1993. *Race and class.* London: Bookmarks.

Cherlin, A. J. 1992. *Marriage, divorce, remarriage.* Cambridge, MA: Harvard University Press.

Chesser, B. J. 1980. Analysis of wedding rituals: An attempt to make weddings more meaningful. *Family Relations* 29; 204–209.

Clark, John. 1993. Bride and joy. *Premiere* (March): 108.

Cole, Harriette. 1995. *Jumping the broom: The African American wedding planner*. New York: Henry Holt.

College Board and Educational Testing Service. 1997. College board entrance examinations. Princeton, New Jersey.

Coontz, Stephanie. 1997. *The way we really are*. New York: Basic Books.

———. 1992. *The way we never were*. New York: Basic Books.

Currie, D. 1993. "Here comes the bride": The making of a "modern traditional" wedding in western culture. *Journal of Comparative Family Studies* 24, 3; 403–421.

Debord, Guy. 1995. *The society of the spectacle*. New York: Zone Books.

Delphy, Christine. 1992. *Familiar exploitation: New analysis of marriage in contemporary western societies*. Polity Press.

———. 1984. *Close to home: A materialist analysis of women's oppression*. London: Hutchinson.

———. 1981. For a materialist feminism. *Feminist Issues* 1.2 (Winter).

———. 1980. *The main enemy*. London: Women's Research and Resource Centre.

Demian. 1997. Partners task force gay and lesbian couples. www.buddybuddy.com

DeVault, Marj. 1993. First comes love. . . : Sociology constructs the family. Presented at the Department of Sociology, Boston University, March.

———. 1991. *Feeding the family: The social organization of caring as gendered work*. Chicago: University of Chicago Press.

Dewitt, Paula M. 1992. The second time around. *American Demographics* (November): pp. 60–63.

Diesenhouse, Susan. 1994. Can she take Priscilla's place at the altar? *New York Times* (October 9): p. 7 Section 3.

Discount Bridal Service. 1997. Press release April 25, Baltimore, MD.

Dogar, Rana. 1997. Here comes the billion dollar bride. *Working Woman* (May): pp. 32–35, 69–70.

Economist. 1996. Many weddings and a discount. *Economist* (January 13): 60.

Ehrenreich, Barbara. 1989. *Fear of falling: The inner life of the middle class*. New York: Pantheon.

Elson, Diane and Ruth Pearson. 1981. *Women's employment and multinationals in Europe*. London: International Specialized Book Service.

Engels, Frederick. 1942. *The origin of the family, private property, and the state in the light of the researches of Lewis H. Morgan*. New York: International.

Enloe, Cynthia. 1993. *The morning after: Sexual politics and the end of the cold war*. Berkeley: University of California Press.

———. 1989. *Bananas, beaches and bases: Making feminist sense of international politics.* Berkeley: University of California Press.

Evans, David T. 1993. *Sexual citizenship: The material construction of sexualities.* New York: Routledge.

Field, Nicola. 1995. *Over the rainbow: Money, class and homophobia.* London: Pluto Press.

Fields, Denise and Alan. 1998. *Bridal gown guide.* Boulder: Windsor Peak Press.

———. 1997. *Bridal bargains.* Boulder: Windsor Peak Press.

Fitzgerald, Kate. 1994. Stewart, Macy's tie knot. *Advertising Age* (May 16): 3, 55.

Foek, Anton. 1997. Sweatshop Barbie. *The Humanitarist* (January–February).

Foley, Barbara and Kathryn London. 1987. Going to the chapel. *American Demographics* (December): 26–31.

Frankenberg, Ruth. 1997. *Displacing Whiteness.* NC: Duke University Press.

Friedman, Sally. 1997. Designing woman: Michele Piccione of Alfred Angelo bridals. *Jewish exponent* (January).

GAO/OGC–97–16 Domain. 1996. Defense of Marriage Act. DC: Government Printing Office.

Gerlin, Andrea. 1994. Your wheels need realignment, and you may now kiss the bride. *Wall Street Journal* (May 17): B1.

Gill, Penny. 1988. Here come the brides! *Stores* (April): 10–24.

Gingrich, Newt. 1996. *Meet the press.* NBC News.

Gite, L. 1992. Do you take this business? *Black Enterprise,* 22 (July 1): 72.

Gramsci, Antonio. 1971. *Selections from the prison notebooks,* translated by Quentin Hoare and Geoffrey Nowell Smith. Newark: International.

Gregory, Marie. 1994. Sandals resorts number one! *Caribbean News Watch* (August 31): 1.

Hacker, Andrew. 1997. *Money: Who has how much and why.* New York: Touchstone.

Haggerty, Alfred. 1993. Coverage is available if wedding bells don't ring. *National Underwriter* (March 15): 15.

Hamlin, Suzanne. 1996. What to give the newlyweds? Just be practical. *New York Times* (June 12): C1:1.

Harman, Moses. 1901. *Institutional marriage.* Chicago: Lucifer.

———. 1883. *Lucifer the lightbearer.* Valley Falls, Kansas.

Helms, Jesse. 1996a. The defense of marriage act. Senate. *Congressional Quarterly,* September 9.

———. 1996b. Senate proceedings. *Congressional Record,* September 9.

Hennessy, Rosemary. 1996a. Lesbians in late capitalism: Queer subjects, class acts. *Das Argument* (Fall).

———. 1996b. Ambivalence as alibi: On the materiality of late capitalist myth in *The Crying Game* and cultural theory. *Genders* 24 (Summer).

———. 1995. Subjects, knowledges. . . And all the rest: Speaking for what? In *Who can speak?: Authority and critical identity*. Edited by Judith Roof and Robyn Wiegman. Urbana: University of Illinois Press.

———. 1994–95. Queer visibility in commodity culture. *Cultural Critique* 29 (Winter).

———. 1994. Incorporating queer theory on the left. In *Marxism in the Postmodern Age*. Edited by Antonio Callari, Stephen Cullenberg, Carole Beweiner. New York: Guilford. 1994.

———. 1993a. *Materialist feminism and the politics of discourse*. New York: Routledge.

———. 1993b. Women's lives/Feminist knowledge: Feminist standpoint as ideology critique. *Hypatia* 8.1: 14–34.

Hennessy, Rosemary and Chrys Ingraham, eds. 1997. *Materialist Feminism: A Reader in Class, Difference and Women's Lives*. New York: Routledge.

———. 1992. Putting the heterosexual order in crisis. *Mediations* 16.2: 17–23.

Hennessy, Rosemary and Rajeswari Mohan. 1989. The construction of woman in three popular texts of empire: Towards a critique of materialist feminism. *Textual Practice* 3.3: 323–59.

Heywood, Ezra. 1876. *Cupid's yokes*. Princeton, Mass.: Co-operative Publishing Company.

Hochschild, Arlie. 1985. *The managed heart*. Berkeley: University of California Press.

Holloron, Gerry. 1998. People: Gingrich's youngest daughter marries businessman. *Morning News Tribune* (January 25).

Holstein, William J., Brian Palmer, Shahid Ur-Rehman, and Timothy M. Ito. 1996. Santa's sweatshop. *U.S. News & World Report* (December 16).

Hoogasian, Cindy. 1994. Fairy tales do come true. *Florist* 27 (May 1): 40.

hooks, bell. 1992. *Black looks: Race and representation*. Boston: South End Press.

———. 1990. *Yearning: Race, gender and cultural politics*. Boston: South End Press.

———. 1984. *Feminist theory: From margin to center*. Boston, MA: South End Press.

———. 1981. *Ain't I a woman: Black women and feminism*. Boston: South End Press.

Hoover's. 1998. Business online. www.hoovers.com

Illouz, Eva. 1997. *Consuming the romantic utopia: Love and the cultural contradictions of capitalism*. Berkeley: University of California Press.

In Style. 1997. Celebrity weddings. *In Style* (February): 125.

Ingraham, Chrys. 1996. Systemic pedagogy: Activating sociological thinking. *International Journal of Sociology and Social Policy* (Fall).

———. 1994. The heterosexual imaginary: Feminist sociology and theories of gender. *Sociological Theory* 12.2 (July): 203–219.

———. 1992. *Out of print, out of mind: Toward a materialist feminist theory of censorship and suppression.* Dissertation. Syracuse University.

Ingraham, Chrys and Rosemary Hennessy, eds. 1997. *Materialist feminism: A reader in class, difference and women's lives.* New York: Routledge.

Jackson, Stevi. 1996. Heterosexuality and feminist theory. In *Theorising Heterosexuality.* Edited by Diane Richardson. Buckingham: Open University Press.

Jary, David and Julia Jary. 1991. *The Harper Collins dictionary of sociology.* New York: Harper Collins.

Jewelers' Circular-Keystone. 1996. Diamond sales hit record. New York: Chilton.

Johnson, Bradley. 1992. Will couples say I do to Disney? *Advertising Age* (March 30): 52.

Katz, Jonathan Ned. 1996. *The invention of heterosexuality.* New York: Plume.

Kaufman, Joanne. 1995. Buy, buy love. *Ladies Home Journal* 112, (June 1): 100.

Kellner, Douglas. 1995. Cultural studies, multiculturalism and media culture. In *Media Culture.* Edited by Douglas Kellner. New York: Routledge.

Kincaid, Jamaica. 1989. *A small place.* New York: Plume Books.

Kuczynski, A. 1998. Arm candy: A sign of the times. *New York Times* (October 3): 9.1.

Lee, Vera. 1994. *Something old, something new.* Naperville, Ill.: Sourcebooks.

Lenin, V. I. 1966. *The emancipation of women.* New York: International Publishers.

Linsen, Mary Ann. 1991. Decorated cakes—the icing on bakery sales. *Progressive Grocer* (February): 117–120.

Lipton, Lauren. 1992. TV with a hitch in it: Wedding bells are ringing on at least a dozen series this season. *Los Angeles Times* (April 14): 1.

Los Angeles Times. 1995. Off the cuff; Her job has the ring of romance (January 26): E-4.

Macionis, John. 1997. *Sociology.* New York: Prentice-Hall.

MacDonald, George. 1972. *Fifty years of freethought.* New York: Arno Press.

Marx, Karl. 1977. *Capital.* Translated by Ben Fowkes. New York: Vintage.

———. 1972. *The grundisse,* edited by David McLellan. New York: Harper & Row.

———. 1970a. *Capital, vol. 1.* New York: International Publishers.

———. 1970b. *A contribution to the critique of political economy.* New York: International Publishers.

———. 1963. *The eighteenth brumaire of Louis Bonaparte.* New York: International.

———. 1844. *Contribution to the critique of Hegel's philosophy of law.* Moscow: International Publishers.

Marx, Karl and Frederick Engels. 1988. *The communist manifesto.* New York: Norton.

———. 1976a. *Collected works.* New York: International.

———. 1976b. *The German ideology.* New York: International.

Maynard, Mary and June Purvis, eds. 1995. *(Hetero)sexual politics.* London: Taylor & Francis.

McMurdy, Deirdre. 1993. Banking on bliss. *McLean's* 106 (June 28): 40–41.

McWilliams, Michael. 1996. Weddings are the icing for the May sweeps. *The Detroit News* (May 16): 7.

Mehta, Stephanie. 1996. Bridal superstores woo couples with miles of gowns and tuxes. *Wall Street Journal* (February 14): B1–B2.

Mieher, Stuart. 1993. Great expectations: the stork is a guest at more weddings. *Wall Street Journal* (April 6): A1, A6.

Mies, Maria. 1986. *Patriarchy and accumulation on a world scale: Women in the international division of labor.* London: Zed.

Miller, Cyndee. 1995. 'Til death do they part. *Marketing News* 29, (March 27): 1–5.

Modern Bride. 1996. *The bridal market retail spending study: A $35 billion market for the 90's.* New York: Primedia.

———. 1994. *The bridal market retail spending study: A $35 billion market for the 90's.* New York: Primedia.

Mogelonsky, Marcia. 1994. The world of weird insurance. *American Demographics* (December): 37.

Monsarrat, Ann. 1973. *And the bride wore. . . ; the story of the white wedding.* New York: Follett.

Morrison, Toni. 1970. *The bluest eye.* New York: Pocket Books.

Nagel, Bart and Karen Huff. 1997. Something old, something new. *Might* (March/April): 43–51.

National Center for Health Statistics. 1997. www.cdc.gov/nchswww

Nelton, Sharon. 1990. What she does for love. *Nation's Business* 78 (June): 18–26.

Nibley, MaryBeth. 1994. Editor to divorce herself from long career of helping brides. *Los Angeles Times* (December 7): D–7.

Niebuhr, Gustav. 1998. Just tell us which sin. *New York Times* (September 27): 5.

O'Barr, William M. 1994. *Culture and the ad: Exploring otherness in the world of advertising.* Boulder: Westview Press.

Omvedt, Gail. 1986. Patriarchy: The analysis of women's oppression. *Insurgent Sociologist* 13.3: 30–50.

Oppenheimer, Nicholas. 1998. Chairman's statement. *Annual Report.* De Beers.

Parker, E. 1995. Federal report finds: Blacks median age younger than whites, women older than men. *Los Angeles Sentinel* (June 7): A–4.

Partners Task Force for Gay & Lesbian Couples. 1997. (January 31). www.buddybuddy.com/mar-feda.html

Paul, James and Murray Schwartz. 1961. *Federal censorship: Obscenity in the mail.* New York: Free Press.

People. 1998. I finally found someone: Streisand and Bolin wed.

———. 1997. When couples have children. (June 1): 169.

———. 1995a. Cowie as Hollywood's wedding consultant. (June 1): 136.

———. 1995b. Wedding shockers. (June 1): 125.

———. 1991. Once upon a time . . . the world fell in love with a dashing Prince and his enchanting bride. (July 30): 23.

Pereira, A. 1996. Toy business focuses more on marketing and less on new ideas. *Wall Street Journal* (December 10): A1.

Powell, Rachel. 1991. It's one party even the recession can't spoil. *New York Times* (June 23): 10.

PR Newswire. 1998. www.prnewswire.com

Press, Eyal. 1996. Sweatshopping. *Z Magazine.*

Rapping, Elayne. 1995. A bad ride at Disney World. *The Progressive* (November): 36–39.

Raub, Deborah Fineblum. 1994. Saying "I do" without going broke. Gannett News Service (February 23).

Reinholz, Mary. 1996. Spring '96 bridal planner/Jewelry gifts for the wedding party. *Newsday* (February 18): 5.

Reynolds, Christopher. 1992. Overseas marriage ceremonies have a certain 'ring' for some couples matrimony: Wedding travel specialists help Americans exchange vows in foreign destinations. *Los Angeles Times* (May 17): 2.

Rich, Adrienne. 1980. Compulsory heterosexuality and lesbian existence. *Signs* 5 (Summer): 631–60.

Richardson, Diane, ed. 1996. *Theorising heterosexuality*. Buckingham: Open University Press.

Robey, Bryant. 1990. Wedding-bell blues chime as marriage markets shift. *Adweek's Marketing Week* (June 25): 10, 12.

Rosen, Margery. 1995. I can't count on him. *Ladies Home Journal* (June): 21–23.

Ross, Andrew. 1997. *No sweat*. New York: Verso.

Rubin, Elizabeth. 1997. An army of one's own: In Africa, nations hire a corporation to wage war. *Harper's* (February): 44–56.

Sailer, David. 1997. Lifting the veil: A special report. A whitepaper published by Union of Needleworkers and Textile Employees, New York.

Salkever, Alex. 1995. Let's get married. *Hawaii Business* (May 1): 45.

Schifrin, Matthew. 1991. The newlywed game. *Forbes* (September 2): 85–86.

Schoen, Robert. 1988. *Modeling multigroup populations*. New York: Plenum.

Schoolman, Judith. 1997. Love may be free, but it's getting progressively more expensive to tie the knot. *Reuters Business Report* (June 4).

Schwartz, Mary Ann, and Barbara M. Scott. 1997. *Marriages & families: Diversity and change*. New York: Prentice-Hall.

Sears, Hal D. 1977. *The sex radicals: Free love in high Victorian America*. Lawrence: Regents Press of Kansas.

Seidman, Steven. 1993. Identity and politics in a postmodern gay culture: Some conceptual and historical notes. In *Fear of a queer planet*, edited by Michael Warner. Minneapolis: University of Minnesota Press.

———. 1992. *Embattled eros*. New York: Routledge

———. 1991. *Romantic longings*. New York: Routledge.

Sewell, Dan. 1998. Blacks' buying power outpaces national trend. *Philadelphia Inquirer* (July 30): C2.

Sherwin, Nina. 1995. Clone this idea: Wedding consultant. *Executive Female* 18 (November 1): 30.

Smith, Dorothy. 1990a. *The conceptual practices of power: A feminist sociology of knowledge*. Boston: Northeastern Press.

———. 1990b. *Texts, facts, and femininity*. New York: Routledge.

———. 1987. *The everyday world as problematic: Toward a feminist sociology*. Boston: Northeastern University Press.

———. 1975. An analysis of ideological structures and how women are excluded: Considerations for academic women. *Canadian Review of Sociology and Anthropology* 12 (4): 131–54.

———. 1974. Women's perspective as a radical critique of sociology. *Sociological Inquiry* 44: 73–90.

Smythers, Ruth. 1894. Instruction and advice for the young bride. *The Madison Institute Newsletter* (Fall): 4.

Spears, Dawn. 1995. Till debt do us part. *Kiplinger's Personal Finance Magazine* 49 (May 1): 64–66.

Spindler, Amy. 1998. The bride that ate Hollywood: New movies, TV shows and 5-pound bridal magazines prove how much we love weddings. *New York Times* (September 2): 9.1.

St. Louis Dispatch. 1997. Some targets of Baptist's Disney boycott (June 19): 08A.

Starr, Kenneth. 1998. *Starr Report.* New York: Prima Publishing.

Steurle, C. Eugene. 1995. *Economic effects of health care reform.* New York: AEI Press.

Stevenson, Brenda. 1996. *Life in black and white: Family and community in the slave south.* New York: Oxford.

Stewart, Martha, and Christopher Baker. 1988. *The wedding planner.* New York: Crown Publications.

Stewart, Martha, Elizabeth Hawes, Christopher P. Baker, and Chris Baker. 1987. *Weddings.* New York: Clarkson Potter.

Stoehr, Taylor. 1979. *Free love in America: A documentary history.* New York: AMS Press, Inc.

Stolcke, Verena. 1983. Women's labours: The naturalisation of social inequality and women's subordination. In *Of Marriage and the Market: Women's Subordination Internationally and Its Lessons.* Edited by Kate Young, Carol Wolkowitz, and Roslyn McCullagh. London: Routledge.

Storey, John. 1993. *An introductory guide to cultural theory and popular culture.* Athens, GA: University of Georgia Press.

Strauss, Larry A. 1994. Wedlock has its benefits. Gannett News Service.

Thompson, Roger. 1990. Romancing a $30 billion market. *Nation's Business* 78 (June): 18–21.

Toalston, Art. 1998. Boycott may be taking its toll. *The Ethics and Religious Liberty Commission of the Southern Baptist Convention* (April 27): www.erlc.com/Culture/Disney

Torrant, Julie. 1998. For better or worse: Marriage in commodity culture. Unpublished manuscript.

Toussaint, A. 1997/1998. Dangerous liaisons: Rewriting history for Hollywood's classic couples. *Bride's* (Winter): 421.

Travel Weekly. 1996. Romantic places: 1996 Supplement: Honeymoon vacations (November 7): 8–12.

Tucker, B., and C. Kernan. 1995. *The decline in marriage among African Americans.* New York: Russell Sage Foundation.

Urban League. 1996. *The state of black America.* New York: Astoria Graphics.

U.S. Bureau of the Census. 1996. *Statistical abstracts of the U.S.* Washington, DC: Government Printing Office.

U.S. Department of Commerce. 1994. Washington, DC: Government Printing Office.

U.S. Department of Labor. 1996. Three apparel companies added to labor department's Trendsetters' List. Press release, March 27.

VanEvery, Jo. 1996. Heterosexuality and domestic life. In *Theorising heterosexuality.* Edited by Diane Richardson. Buckingham: Open University Press.

Walby, Sylvia. 1989. *Theorizing patriarchy.* London: Blackwell.

———. 1987. *Patriarchy at work.* Minneapolis: University of Minnesota Press.

Watts, Christina. 1994. Here comes the money: Fashioning a bridal consulting business. *Black Enterprise* (July 31): 16.

Wilkinson, Sue and Celia Kitzinger, eds. 1993. *Heterosexuality; A feminism and psychology reader.* London: Sage Publications.

Williamson, Christine and Mercedes M. Cardona. 1996. Institutions like possible Mattel/Hasbro marriage. *Pensions and investments* (February 5): 1.

Willis, Susan. 1991. *A primer for daily life.* New York: Routledge.

With, Tatiana. 1996. Unveiling wedding hell. *Boston Globe* (March 21): 85:1.

Wittig, Monique. 1992. *The straight mind.* Boston: Beacon Press.

Wright, John W. 1999. *The New York Times almanac 1999 (annual).* New York: Penguin Books.

Zavarzadeh, Mas'ud. 1991. *Seeing films politically.* Albany: SUNY Press.

Zuber, Amy. 1994. Time Inc.'s *People* person. *Folio* (December 15): 70, 72.

Photo Permissions

Page 5: Three women, one with wedding cake hat. Photo provided by and reprinted with permission of *Times Union*/Albany NY. Copyright © 1996.

Page 6: Photo of Dennis Rodman in wedding dress by Peter Morgan. Copyright © 1996 by Reuters and Archive Photos. Reprinted with permission of Archive Photos.

Page 35: Princess Grace in prayer. Reprinted with permission of CORBIS/Bettmann.

Page 37: Princess Diana as a bride. Reprinted with permission of CORBIS/Hulton-Deutsch Collection.

Page 40: Fairy-tale wedding gown. Photo provided by Mary's Bridal of P.C. Mary's, Inc. Reprinted with permission of Mary's Bridal of P.C. Mary's, Inc.

Page 41: Wedding gown in bridal store. Collection of the author.

Page 42: Wedding gowns in thrift store window. Collection of the author.

Page 43: Bridal gown store out of business. Collection of the author.

Page 48: Sweatshop. Reprinted with permission of UNITE, Union of Needletrades, Industrial, and Textile Employees, AFL-CIO, CLC.

Page 48: UNITE workers. Reprinted with permission by UNITE, Union of Needletrades, Industrial, and Textile Employees, AFL-CIO, CLC.

Page 67: Colgate ad.

Page 91: Bridal magazines in bookstore. Collection of the author.

Page 96: Girl dressed as Barbie Bride for Halloween. Collection of the author.

Page 96: Bridal doll in store window. Collection of the author.

Page 103: "Left at the Altar," by Virginia Breen and Corky Siernaszko. Copyright © *New York Daily News*, I.P. Reprinted with permission.

Page 163: Two men on top of a wedding cake. Photo provided by and reprinted with permission of *Times Union*/Albany NY. Copyright © 1996.

Index